A Challenge

Multi talented, Manipal Aruna Kumari, is a first A-Grade blind veena artist of A.I.R. (Prasara Bharathi, New Delhi). She had lost her complete vision by retinal detachments and also the strength in fingers by arthritis, at the tender age of six years! These are the main requirements for rendering and mastering veena. She has acquired good experience in veena rendering, Carnatic classical vocal music and in playing violin. She had a brilliant academic carrier in these and is also a post graduate in Sociology. She had her advanced studies in veena rendering technique under the world-famous Vainika, Thrissur A.Ananthapadmanabhan, A-Top veena artist of A.I.R. Thrissur and has already conducted few hundreds of veena concerts, few accompaniments to Bharatha Naatyams, vocal concerts, fusion music (laya-vaddya) etc,. Recently, music students and music lovers are losing interest in this most melodious naada of Divine veena, the perfect and the first of the best of all music instruments.

Veena is our National emblem for all fine arts! This is a timely publication, in view of reviving the past glory and high reputation for veena, which is her mission and vision!

ISBN 979-8-88883-687-3

Divine Veena Science

(A Study) by
Manipal Aruna Kumari
Sangeetha Kachchapi
4-22 D. Prashanti House, Vidyaratna Nagar,
Manipal, Udupi - 576 104. Karnataka.
Ph.: 94492 06379, & 9480227823.

Co-Author:
Prof. V. Shama Bhat
Retd. H.O.D., Dental Materials,
College of Dental Surgery Manipal and
Yenepoya University, Mangalore - India
Ph.: 94802 27823
Mail: shamabhatv@gmail.com

Contents

Foreword: By Sri A. Anantha Padmanabhan 7

Introduction by Author...9

Chapter - 1   Supreme of the Musical Instruments...........................15

Chapter - 2   History and Evolution of Veena 21

Chapter - 3   Saraswathi or Gayathri Veena...................................32

Chapter - 4   Science of Saraswathi Veena......................................41

Chapter - 5   Veena Rendering Methods and Styles 55

Chapter - 6   Veena Rendering Specialities-Thaanams and Gamakas...65

Chapter - 7   Veena Naada-Yoga-Salvation....................................73

Chapter - 8   Varieties of Veenas and String Instruments...............81

Chapter - 9   Famous Vainikas 97

Chapter - 10   Raaga Identification and Analysis...........................112

Chapter - 11   Divine Veena: Its Present Status.............................115

Bibliography 121

Foreword

Veena is one of the most ancient instruments, which has undergone many innovations since, pre-Vedic periods, until Thulajendra finalized the structure to the present, Saraswathi (Gayathri) Veena of twenty-four frets and seven strings. This is a most divine and perfect musical instrument, Sarva Raaga- maya and Sarva Deva-maya. Veena has purity of tone, deep sonorous overtones, reverberating undertones and tremulous gamakas bewitching the listeners and is the closest to human voice. Veena was the most revered stringed instrument at the time of music Trinities and even until the last century. However, veena is losing its earlier glories and importance due to the invasions by the modern electronic gadgets and technologies. I, very much appreciate my student Miss Aruna Kumari, for collecting many, very useful information arranging them systematically and publishing. The material is well-balanced, presented in an attractive manner with relevant diagrams and has good flow to engross the readers. This is perhaps a unique book, covering the essential knowledge of veena and its techniques required for every veena student. It is also useful to the music students, teachers, as well as all music lovers. The usefulness of this book was soon recognized by the music (veena) students and music-lovers in Karnataka.

I have to thank her again for obliging my request of bringing this English edition, which will be very useful for extensive range of readers in whole India, especially in Kerala, Tamilnadu, and Andhra States. This edition is enriched with some more interesting information. I hope this excellent work and the efforts taken, will serve the mission and vision of the author, that is, to revive the

earlier popularity, respect and the glorious status for Veena and Vainikas.

My best wishes,

Rageshri,   **A. Anantha Padmanabhan**
Thrissur.   Rtd.A-TOP AIR Vainika,
                                                                Thrissur.

* * * * *

Introduction

This book is an attempt to revive the past glory and reputations of the Saraswathi Veena, the most melodious Divine string musical instrument. This is the perfect musical instrument with all the four basic pillars of music (chathurdandis), namely, shruthi, rhythm (laya or thala), swara (notes), and playable any raga. It is the King of all musical instruments.

Veena is one of the most ancient musical instruments. In the Vedic period, the human spine, was named as Veena Dandi, and was played during religious functions, Yajnas and Yaagas. Many innovative changes took place, from the single stringed Veena of the pre-Vedic period, until, Sri Thulajendra finalized the structure to the present Saraswathi or Gayathri Veena of 24 frets and 7 (4+3) strings. The sacred Gayathri mantra has 24 letters. This structure of the present Veena, is close to the anatomy (and resemblance) of the human gross body. Our spine, on average, has about 24 vertebrae, of which, 5 are lumbar, 12 are dorsal, and 7 are cervicals. In Veena (second string - mandra panchama), the first 5 are of low pitch (mandra sthayi), the next 12 frets are of middle pitch (madhya sthayi) and last 7 frets, are of high pitch (thara sthayi) respectively. Vibrations of Veena strings, follow all the laws of vibrations of stretched strings, resonance energy transfer, overtones, undertones, harmonics, etc. Surprisingly, the functions are rather comparable to those of our invisible subtle body (Sookshma Sharira). The invisible spiritual centers are identified at different locations The Mooladhara chakra is at Meru, where sound energy is generated and Kundalini is supposed to be present. These have higher energy values as these move to Ajna chakra at the Veena Bridge. These finally are transmitted to Sahasrara inside the resonator, below the bridge, where it is enriched with the overtones and undertones and its music resonates,

producing spiritual experience of bliss. "Veena has a purity of tone, deep sonorous overtones, reverberating undertones, and tremulous gamakas, bewitching the listeners and is closest to the human voice. The most melodious naada of Veena rendering, resonates within the hearts and minds of the listeners and makes them forget themselves in the celestial bliss, which is "Ananda Rasa Samadhi!"

Veena was the most revered instrument at the time of music Trinities (Sri Thyagaraja, Shyama Shastry, and Muthu Swamy Dixithar, of the 19th century), and even until the last century, to the period of Veena maestros, Veenai Dhanammal, S. Bala chandar, Mysuru Veene Sheshanna, and many others. Many Vainikas were honoured by Kings as Royal Musicians (Asthaana Vidwans) and supported by many rich people.

According to Saranga Deva, (in "Sangeeta Ratnakara") Veena is 'Sarva Deva maya' celestial instrument, since all the forms of Gods and Goddesses are supposed to be present in the various parts of the Veena. According to sage Yajnavalkya, even seeing or just touching veena, one can get rid of all evils and became elligible for Moksha!

"Darshane sparshane chaasya bhoga swargapavargade etc"

It is also unique, Sarva raga maya Veena as infinite varieties of ragas of any type (Carnatic, Hindustani, any Western or Eastern styles, classical or light music, at any pitch or Shruthi, with single tuning! It is a perfectly ideal musical instrument. Veena is the standard instrument for checking the correctness of swara sthanas (pitch or frequency) of other notes! Dixithar has composed a krithi "Kanja Dalayathaksi" in "Kamala Manohari" ragam including the three seed letters Ka-Ja-Tha (out of 12 symbolic petals of heart lotus). This is the key krithi (Sadhaka manthra) to achieve skill in all fine arts.

Special features of Veena rendering techniques leading to its enchanting melodious music notes are, many varieties of Thaanams and rich gamakas (without which Veena concert is said to be incomplete!). The Structure of Veena is best suited for playing Thaanam and gamakas.

Veena is our National Emblem of all fine arts.

However Veena is losing fast, it's past glory and popularity, perhaps due to the impact of modern electronic gadgets and otherwise busy present students and employed persons. The number of good Vainikas and Veena students is dwindling rapidly, due to lack of public support and program organizing sponsors.

At this rate, it is afraid that the Divine Veena music may vanish in the near future. This is an invaluable loss to the world of music and our Indian Heritage.

However recently, in India and Western countries people are showing good interest to study and follow Indian philosophies like Yoga, ancient scripts (Vedas. Upanishads), classical music, and instruments (Veena, Mridangam, Thabla Ghatam, etc), classical dances (Bharat Natyams, Mohini Attam, Koochupudi, Kathak) etc. Perhaps this is to experience spiritual bliss and to relieve them from mental tensions caused by their busy life schedule.

At the age of six years I lost my complete vision due to retinal detachment by pathological myopia. Rheumatic arthritis caused weak distorted fingers. Interest in the spiritual field and singing Sri Sai Bhajans, made me to study Carnatic classical music and Veena playing. My parents and family members supported me to study Veena aeven though it is the most complicated instrument and impossible to attain good skill without strong fingers and vision. But I took a challenging bold decision to study Divine Veena

I commenced my music studies with Carnatic classical music under Vidwan Udupi Vasudeva Bhat (later Suralu Parameshwara Bhat and Mrs. Lalitha Ballal), and learnt violin playing from Vidwan Raghavendra Bhat. Viidushi, late, Mrs. Laksmi Iyengar trained me excellently, in Veena playing techniques, with motherly affection and devotion which

secured me precious Vidushi title. The thirst for learning the best techniques, was supported by scholar ships and by great Veena Maestro of the present time, Sri A.Anantha Padmanabhan, A-Top Vainika, of All India Radio, Thrissure, I was attending classes at his house, (one week, in every month) for about ten years! These secured me the coveted "A-Grading" from Prasara Bharathi, New Delhi. I am very gratefull for his guidance and blessings.

During this period, I secured M.A. in Sociology from Mysore University, and training in the spiritual (Shri Chakram) field by Dr. P. V. Sesha Sai of Hyderabad. I also performed a few hundred public Veena concerts (at Mysore, Chennai, Hyderabad, Madhya Pradesh, Maha Rashtra, Kerala, etc), and many All India Radio Veena concerts at Thrissur and Mangalore. Now I am devoting my entire time for the cause of Veena.

I do not have any words to express my gratitude to my beloved mother, late, Mrs. Himavathi S. Bhat, for devoting her entire time and energy to bring me to this level. She had to prepare the notes, help to practise Veena, violin and classical vocal musics. These are in addition to assisting and inspiring me to attend classes. My father, a very senior Professor and all family members have fully supported me in these adventures.

In the year, 2013 my father suggested preparing a book, briefly highlighting all the information about Veena to promote its popularity. We enjoyed editting the large information collected from many sources. We added many applications of modern science and our own explanations.

To know the response of music lovers, few copies of "Sarva Bhouma Veena Vijnana" in Kannada language was printed and distributed. This work was very much appreciated with feedbacks. Many suggested to prepare the same in English to benefit larger number of readers throughout the world.

To create more interest, and benefit for the music lovers, teachers and students, we have briefly included most of all available information regarding Veena with required details.

Authors' wish to thank especially, Dr. Mrs. Hemalatha Shivarama Bhat, Miss Shamathmika and Miss Ramathmika for assisting in preparing this manuscript.

The authors are grateful to Notion publishers, Chennai, for accepting publication and promotion.

Manipal Aruna Kumari

* * * * *

Chapter - 1

Supreme of the Musical Instruments

Veena has a very long history much earlier than the Vedic period (3500-2500 B.C.) There were many varities of string music instruments at that time and all these were named as veenas. There are many references to veenas in the Vedas and Upanishads. Veena was worshipped as an incarnation of the Goddess of knowledge (vidya), Saraswathi. Surprisingly, the spinal cord was named as veena dandi in the Vedas. Incidentally, the present 24 frets-7 stringed Saraswathi veena has its structure very close to our spinal cord! Even at that time, people had recognized the value of its melodious sound, closest to the human voice. Veena concert is so much pleasing; it creates peace and internal happiness or bliss and releases all the internal stresses and strains in the mind. Interested listeners, while concentrating on the veena- naada, forget themselves for a while and experience the celestial bliss or lose themselves in the ocean of bliss i.e. Rasa Samaadhi or Bhaava Samaadhi! In every religious functions and activities on auspicious days, festivals, Yaagas, and Yajnas, veena concerts used to be an inseparable and unavoidable part.

It is believed that for the harmonious development of the mind of the baby in the womb, a pregnant woman should be kept in the unexcited and tension-free state of mind. For this, she is made frequently to listen to veena recitals during the pregnancy period. Even now, at least on the day of the religious function "Seemantha or baby shower", performed in the seventh month of pregnancy, veena concerts are held, in such occasions in Andhra, Karnataka, Thamilnadu, and Kerala. This is supposed to assist the child to becomie pious, sathvik and develop ideal personality.

People considered veena as the best music instrument, throughout the Vedic and historic periods. Great musician, Parameshwara has called veena as Maharani (queen) of all the musical instruments!

Sarva Deva-maya, Divine veena

Veena is considered as a very sacred divine music instrument in the history and glorious culture of our country. The present twenty four frets and seven strings veena is the best and perfect musical instrument. On special occasions and festivals, veena concerts are still conducted in temples by the temple authorities or by some sponsors mostly during the Navaraathri festivals. These are for worshipping of Energy Goddesses (Adi Shakthi) for nine days in many forms. Many veena concerts are held especially in the temples and other places in Mysore and South Indian states. This festival refers to worshipping the three energy divinity forms, Maha Kali, during the first three days, Maha Laxmi during the next three days and Maha Saraswathi in the last three days, respectively. During the last three days, Saraswathi pooja is performed in many houses. Veena, along with some books, is placed in their prayer rooms, in front of the Saraswathi's idol or photo and worshipped by the music teachers, with the students, along with music and veena renderings. Goddess Saraswathi is considered as a form of the deity for knowledge (vidya) and fine-arts. She is always depicted in idols and pictures, holding her veena, Kachchapi. (Goddess Maathangi was said to be playing Veena, –in "Durga Saptha shathi").

It is presumed that many forms of Gods and Goddesses are present in the various parts of Divine veena and bless the Vainikas rendering the enchanting celestial music, making the listeners to achieve highest form of bliss or Rasa-Samaadhi. Saaranga Deva in his "Sangeetha Rathnakara" had praised the divinity and the importance of the Saraswathi veena as,

"Darshanae sparshanae chaasya, bhoga swargapavargadae |
Punitho vipra hathyadi pathakee pathitham janam ||
Dandah Shambhu, Umaa thanthri, kakubhi Kamalaapathihi |

Indira pathrika, Brahma thumbum, naabhi Saraswathee ||
Dorako Vasukih, jeeva Sudhaamshu, Saarika Ravihi |
Sarva Deva mayi thasmaath veenium sarva mangalaa ||"

"By just seeing or touching the veena, one will get peac and happiness in this world as well as later in the next worlds, (Iha and Para). This removes the effect of all the bad, even criminal acts, from the mind and purifies the person. Many deities present in the various parts of veena are, Shiva (Shambhu) in the Dandi (hollow finger board), Paarvathi (Uma) in the strings, Vishnu in the bridge, Laxmi in the rekhu (pathrika), Brahma in the resonator (kuda), Saraswathi in the navel (Nabhi), Vaasuki (serpent king, seat of Mahaa-Vishnu) in the knobs (biradai), Chandra (moon) in the jeevala (life-strings), and Sun in the 24 mansions (sarika-spaces in between the frets)"

One pious devotee of veena, Mr. Nataraja, from Malleshwaram (Bangalore) has prepared a huge wooden veena about fifteen feet in length, and carved all the above deities in their respective positions. This is exhibited to the visitors at the Sri Jagadguru Mutt of Sri Sharadamba Temple, at Sringeri (Karnataka), which is one of the centers of energy (Shakthi) deities in India, established by Sri Shankaracharya.

Sarva raaga-maya veena

Indian classical music has been evolved in a very systematic scientific manner enabling the artists to sing or render, enriching them with aalapana, thaanam, swaraprasthara, neraval etc, according to their own imaginations (or mano-dharmas). The basic components of any music are shruthi (drone considered as the mother), laya or rhythm (as father), and ability to render any swaras notes, and raagas. Veena perhaps is the only one of the rare stringed musical instruments, which has all these components. It is possible to render any of the 72 melakartha raagas of Venkatamukhi's classification, their janya raagas and also any other infinite varieties of raagas obtained by the permutations and combinations of the various notes. It is also possible to enrich them with all varieties of thaanams and gamakas. This gives

most melodius, unexciting, blissfull music. That is why; it is the perfect musical instrument, the King or Queen of all instruments!

The most attractive and appealing part of the veena concert is the technique of rendering varieties of thaanams. There is no veena concert without thaanams. Design of Saraswathi veena is the most suitable for rendering the melodious thaanams and inclusion of all gamakas in all raagas. These are its specialities. These enrichments with thaanams and gamakas make the audience spell- bound!

The well known music Trinities (Thrimurthys), Sri Muthu Swamy Dikshitar, Naada Brahma Sri Thyagaraja and Sri Shyama Shastry (18th-19th century) were very famous vainikas, musicians and krithi composers (Vaggeyakaras). They were well-aware of the superiority of veena in the world of classical music. They used to take the help of veena, to teach and demonstrate complicated parts of the vocal music (with cespecially in Thamilnaadu, even now, are basically vainikas. orrect shruthi, laya, note- positions or swara sancharas etc), which otherwise could not be taught by vocalists clearly. Many of the famous vocalists at that time used to study veena recital first to understand these basics, before they learnt vocal music. Praising the superiority of veena, sage Mathanga -Muni had stated,

"Vainagrahanancha sharire aprakeerthithaha|
Thasyaapi sthaanasya laabartham||"

That is, "veena is the standard reference, for the expert vocalists, to understand the swara-sthaanas and complicated parts of music!"

Since veena is a perfect musical instrument, veena recitals need not even have any accompaniments. However, according to the desire of the present audience, and to please them, vainikas render veena with flutes, mridangam, ghatam, ghanjira, morsing, etc, as accompaniments. Sometimes, especially in fusion music concerts, thabla, keyboard, rhythm-pad, drums, etc., are also used as accompaniments to please the audience.

Supremacy of veena

All the musical instruments of Indian classical music or any other varieties of music instruments in the world can be classified, mainly under three categories that is, string, wind and percussion types. **Surprisingly the Divine Trinities, Brahma, Vishnu and Maheshwaras are associated with these string, wind and percussion music instruments respectively!**

String instruments (thatha vaadyas)

Hundreds of varieties of the string instruments used in India, and other parts of the world can be further classified according to the methods of exciting the strings as;

1. Plucking varieties: thamboora, veena, gottuvadyam, sitar, sarod, etc.
2. Bowing varieties: dilrurba, saarang, violin, etc.

Considering the tonal qualities, melody, and ability to perform all varieties of raagas, and other factors, according to the mano-dharmas, veena was considered as the best in these groups.

Wind instruments (sushira vaadyas)

These also have very long history, like veena. Lord Vishnu has conch (Shankha) in his hand, Lord Gopala Krishna is always found with flute (Venu). But many developments could not be done due to their comparative simplicity. These cannot have the shruthi and laya, in the same instrument like veena. Flute, bansuri, shankha (or conch), naada-swaram, saxophone, shehanai, bugle, harmonium, etc., belong to this type. In this group, flute is selected as the best, considering the ability of rendering many raagas according to the mano-dharma.

Percussions instruments (avanaddha vaadyas)

There are hundreds of varieties of vibrating membrane percussion instruments which are rendered by hand, fingers or striking with rods.

These also have a very long history. Shiva used the Damaru and many of his Ganas use varieties of percussion instruments. The mridanga, thabla, thavil, dolak, drums, chendai, etc, belong to this class. In addition, few other varieties like wooden plates (chitika), earthen pot (ghatam), metal platess (thaala), bells, jagatam, ghanta), etc, are also in use. Considering their melody layam and renderabilities, mridangam was chosen as the best of the percussion instruments.

Considering the richness of tonal qualities, ability to render all varieties of thaanams, gamakas, and raagas with mano-dharmas, inclusion of the three components of the music (shruthi, laya and swaras), veena was chosen as the first among the best of the stringed (thatha), wind (sushira) and percussion (avanaddha) musical instruments. Many more aspects, supporting this statement are explained in this book.

Shri Adi Shankaracharya, in his famous composition "Meenakshi Pancha Rathnam", has praised Goddess, Madurai Meenakshi, as **"veena, venu, mridanga vaadya rasike."** In this also veena is the first of the bests!

* * * * *

Chapter - 2

History and Evolution of Veena

Veena has a very ancient history going back to the stone ages and even earlier. According to the Indian astronomy, Thula Rashi (Libra in the western Alpha Cygnus), represents hamsa (swan), the seat of Goddess Saraswathi. Swathi means white (shwetha) swan and is also the latter half of the name Saraswathi. The constellation of Swaathi spreads out like the shape of veena. The largest star, Venus in the Thula constellation is also represented in white colour. The present pictures of Saraswathi are shown as seated on white swan or lotus holding the recent version, Gaayathri veena. Scientists and philosophers argue that a Cosmic hissing sound or musical resonating vibrations, like Aum (Pranava-Naada), is pervading and penetrating through the entire Universe, materials and eveything. This sound Aum is the origin or mother of all music!

Primitives of the stone ages and later, in all parts of the world, were basically hunters of animals for food. They were using arrows and bows with strings made of animal guts. Sounds produced by the plucking of the chord of the bow might have been the origin of the string instruments. They might have also discovered that shorter strings and at higher tensions, produce sound of higher pitch, and constructed triangular music instruments, with many strings of different lengths, at different or same tensions. Such an instrument is now known as "harp" in Uruguay, Paraguay, and Venezuela in South America, Mexico in North America, and many European as well as far Eastern countries.

In India, excavations in many places like, Mohenjo-Daro, Harappa, etc., of Indus valley civilization, Iraq and Sumera contemporary

civilizations, revealed the existence of many types of stringed sound producing (musical) instruments during that time. Many later findings from the various stone-carvings, sculptures in the very old caves, and temples in different parts of India, middle, south and south-east Asia, etc, helped to study the evolution of stringed instruments. During these periods, coconut shells, skeletons of heads of monkeys (Kapishira veena), human skull (Runda veena), etc., were used to amplify sound. Hollow bamboo and wooden columns were tied with the strings to get better sound. Multi-stringed bow-shaped instruments also were in practice. Many varieties of string instruments called as Veenas, were in use in the Vedic period. People had clear knowledge of shruthi (drone), laya (rhythm) and notes (swaras) of the musical sounds, which were used for chanting all theVedas with accompanying Veena rendering.

However the major contributions for the detailed studies are available from the Vedic-literatures (Brahmana, Aranyaka, Upanishads), Buddhism and Jainism literatures, Harivamsha, Markandeya and many Puranas, Maha-Kavyas like Ramayana, Bhagavatha, Maha-Bharathas etc,. Literary works and poetic compositions of great personalities like Koutilya, Pathanjali, Bhasa, Shoodraka, Kaalidaasa, Shankaraacharya and many others, contain frequent references to many varieties and names of veenas (stinged), percussion and air-blown instruments. These gradual improvements in the stringed (as well as other music) instruments from the Vedic period until the last five centuries finally resulted in the innovation of the twenty four frets, seven stringed, perfect and best of all the varieties of musical instruments. This is the divine Saraswathi or Gaayathri veena, the Emperor or the Queen of all musical instruments of the world! These veenas had four main parts, shirus (head), udara (dandi), and ambhana (wooden resonator) and of course, strings (thanthris). Veena was considered as very sacred and enjoyed a revered place in the society. Human spinal cord, which has structure very similar to that of present type of veena, was named as veena dandi in Vedas! Man was considered as God's creation, and was called as Deivy veena, or Gaathra veena, which renders vocal

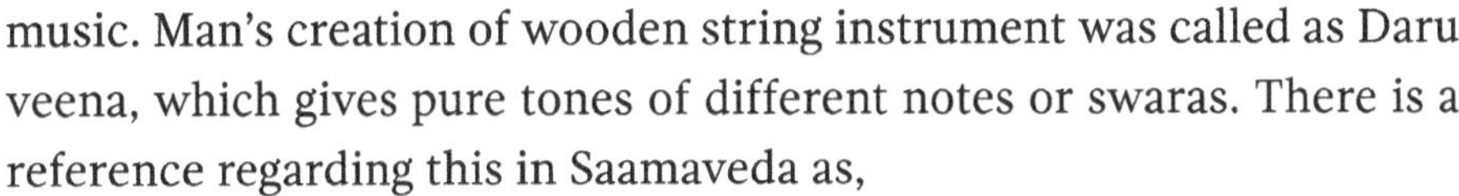

music. Man's creation of wooden string instrument was called as Daru veena, which gives pure tones of different notes or swaras. There is a reference regarding this in Saamaveda as,

"Daaru veena, gaathra veena saathve veena gaana jathishu|
Saamiki gaathra veenathu, thasya shruthi lakshanam||"

In the Vedic period, people were very much aware of the importance and value of music. Musicians commanded good respect in the society and in religous functions. Many were trying to develop string-instruments to play and accompany classical vocal music. Many types of string-music instruments used, were, Bamboo or hollow wooden string instrument known as Kanda veena, the palm-tree-parts variety called as Thaluka veena, string instrument fitted with round gourd (or sore) as Alubu veena, etc. Many other veenas, like, Gaathra, Chala, Randhri, Parivaadini, Kuram, Pitchora, Karthari, Bakur, Oudambari etc, were also very popular. Oudambari veena was played by Yajamaanis (wives) of the persons, while performing Yajnas and Yaagas. In Thitheria Brahmana Upanishath, there is a mention of a huge veena, with hundred strings, known as "Vaana" played by two persons, one being a Brahmin and another Kshathriya!

Many changes in shapes, sizes, structures, number of strings and frets took place during this period to produce better pleasing sounds of various notes and to accompany vocal renderings.. To resonate with the Rigveda chanting techniques in Udaatha (normal), Anudaatha (lower), Svaritha (higher) and Deergha Svaritha (prolonged double Svarithas), with three notes, ni, sa, ri, three frets (or steps) were fixed on the dandi below the strings. Similarly to facilitate chanting of Yajurveda in five notes, da, ni, sa, ri, ga, five frets were fixed and later, for chanting Saamaveda in seven notes, pa, da, ni, sa, ri, ga, ma, (i.e. in saptha swaras) seven frets had to be fixed. These modifications have been done perhaps recently, to use them to play like singing and as accompaniment to vocal chanting music! This introduction of placing of the frets must have indicated the secret of the innovation leading to the

present Saraswathi veena of 24 frets. Now, in many string instruments, like harp, santhoor, swaramandala, etc, different strings are used for different notes. Many instruments contain different numbers of frets, fixed as in veena, or movable as in sitar.

Ancient references to veena

In the great epic Raamayana, Raavana who had mastered music and all branches of knowledge (64 vidyas), prayed vigorously for many years, to please Lord Shiva and get extraordinary powers. But the Lord was not pleased and appeared for a long time. Raavana got very angry and wanted to show his might, by lifting the huge Kailasa Mountain, the abode of Shiva, with his twenty powerful arms. During this attempt, his hands were stuck under the mountain. Raavana realized the fact that his ego was of no use. He realized that to please the God, one should have the devotion, faith and humility (that is, complete surrender to God) and not the ego. He cut his own body, removed some nerves (guts), and held their one ends with his toes and the other ends between his teeth. Using his chest bones as frets, played this as a stringed veena, and rendered Saamagana, as well as music with all seven notes (saptha swaras). This became famous as Shankarabharanam (Shiva's ornament!) raagam. This "King of all raagams" (known as Bilaval in Hindusthani music) is now very much popular in the music of the Western and far Eastern countries. [Note: The present Veenas resemble this standing human visible and invisible (astral) bodies!] These types of Raavana veena or Raavana Hastha veenas, and many other verities of stringed instruments are depicted in the stone sculptured idols of veena artists in the temples of King Hoysala Vishnuvardhan's era, at Belur and Hale- beedu in Karnataka, as well as in many temples and caves of Andhra, Tamilnaadu and Kerala. Raavana was using veena as the emblem (icon) in his (Sri Lanka's) National flag!

Sri Rama's children Lava and Kusha sang the entire Valmiki Ramayana along with rendering of their (Vipanchi) veenas at the King's court!

Many instances are quoted in Ramayana, when veenas are played along with singing, percussion and wind instruments.

Many varieties of stringed musical instruments with different structures and names have been identified by many poets in ancient epics and old devotional verses. All these varieties were different from the present Saraswathi veena but were called as veenas. Many of them are associated with Goddesses, Gods, sages, as well as Kings. Lord Brahma has single stringed veena (thamboora), Naarada used single, four or many stringed Mahathi veena, Thumburu used hundred (or nine) stringed Kalavathi veena, sage Vishwavasu had infinite number stringed Brihathi veena. Hanuman veena (or Chithra veena) had four strings, Rudra veena had six strings, Goddess Lalitha (Para-Shakthi) has nine stringed Vipanchi, Goddess Saraswathi has seven stringed Kachchapi, and Bharatha also had seven stringed veena.

Great sages, Naarada and Thumburu were boasting themselves as expert Vainikas and each one was claiming better than the other. A competition was arranged between them, by the Devas and Lord Hanuman was chosen as the judge by Lord Vishnu. First, Thumburu played Amrithavarshini raagam so powerfully that all the objects on the earth became stationary. Ocean-waves stopped and formation of ice began, and all the animals, flying birds, living beings etc. came to a stand-still. (Actually, this raagam is meant for bringing rains. But great Dikshithar had stopped the heavy continuous rains, by singing Anandaamritha Varshini composition!). Later, Naarada played the famous Punnaaga-varali raagam, equally well, when very good fragrance diffused as expected and restored all of them to their earlier dynamic state. No one could suggest who was better. Lord Hanuman snatched their veenas, removed and threw away all the wax bonded frets (like a mischievous monkey!) and asked them to play again. When theyexpressed their inability Hanuman used a thin bamboo-stick and rendered the veena by sliding the stick with left hand on the strings and plucking with right hand fingers, fantastically, better than Naarada's and Thumburu's performances! Lord Vishnu told, "Vainikas or musicians

should not have ego or superiority complex, but should have humility and devotion". This fretless version is now known as Hanuman veena. The present Gottu vadyam (gottu means sliding in Tamil), or Chithra veena, is like Saraswathi veena without frets but with five main strings.

Veenas in other countries in ancient times

Many varieties of Indian stringed (veena) and other musical instruments appeared in many other neighboring, specially, eastern, countries as the trades, culture, travels, communications and religions spread out at the time of Mouryas, while propagating the Buddhism, i.e.Ahimsa (Non-violence) principles through the Buddhist monks in those countries. It appears that at those ancient times the peace-loving people liked music, musical instruments like veena, classical dances-Bharatha-Natyams etc, In Chinese language thanpoora was called as thanfula, shadja was sha-shiha, shadja-graama was shahu-jiyalan, panchama was penshion etc,. The names of veena was Pipa in China, Biva in Japan, Bana in Egypt, and Soun in Brahma Desh (Burma). Goddes Saraswathi's Kachchapi veena was known as Kadajapi in Philippines at that time! Stone sculptures at Prambanam, Borobudar, Champa, etc places have revealed the existence of the varieties Indian versions of stringed, percussion and wind(blowing) music instruments in these eastern countries. Of course now there are hundreds of verities of stringed etc, instruments, almost in every country.

Veena in Indian history

In the very early pre-historic periods the stringed instruments had curved bow shape with many strings (animal guts) and played by plucking or bowing. Along with the growth of culture, music instruments also developed side by side. This was very much encouraged by the societies and the rulers as revealed by the available literature of the Buddhism and Jainism dominating periods. There were separate departments for teaching systematic chantings of Vedas, vocal music and playing musical instruments of many verities, at many famous education centers (Universities) at that time, at Thakshashila, Varanasi, Nalanda, Thadanthapuri, Vikramashila etc. Specialized music teachers were appointed with respectable salaries and even provided with accommodations! Competitions in playing veenas (stringed) and other instruments were sometimes conducted for selection for the posts, as well as to avail the Kings' recognitions. These have been discovered and studied in great detail with the help of available literature, and hundreds of stone sculptures in many temples, caves and findings during excavations in many historic places in India, and also in Gandhara (Afganisthan), Java, Sumathra, Philippines, China, etc, countries.

It was believed that the veena music could create peace of mind in people but also can calm down even the wild animals! King Udayana of Maurya dynasty used Ghoshavathi veena and is said that he was domesticating wild elephants by veena playing! King Samudra Guptha had released gold coins with boat-shaped multi-stringed Parivadini veena mudra (logo). In south India also, stone sculptures in many temples and caves at Ajantha, Ellora, Amaravathi, Saanchi, Baaadami, Mahabalipuram, Kuppam, Mandagapattu, Naagarjunakonda, Dalavanur etc, reveal the existance of verities stringed, percussion, and wind instruments. Different types of veenas were popular during the regimes of Chalukya, Chola, Pandya, Chera, and Pallava- dynasties. Pallava king Mahendra Verma was also playing Parivadini veena! Musicians commanded good respect in the societies and were encouraged by many rulers with salaries and accommodations!

Innumerable names of stringed instruments (veenas!) are available in the ancient literature such as "Sangeetha Makaranda" of musician Naarada, Hindi dictionary, Padakhanda, etc. Saaranga Deva, Palkurike Somanaatha and many others, also have given the names of many veenas. As mentioned earlier, the structures of these stringed instruments are much different than the present Saraswathi veena. Details, regarding their rendering techniques and structures are not

available. But one thing is definitely a fact, that this large number of names of veenas, is a proof that people of those era liked veena recitals and revered them. Just for curiosity, some names of ancient veenas mentioned are given here:

Haripala in Sangeetha Sudhakara (1175 B.C.) has mentioned the following names of veenas: Brahma (Ekathanthri) veena, Pinaki, Kinneri, Alaapini (alavaani), Kailasa, Aksha-veena.

Palkurike Somanatha in Panditharadhya Charitha (1270 B.C.) There is a mention of thirty-eight names of the verities of veenas at that time: Brahma, Kailasa, Saranga, Koorma, Akasha, Maarga (Vinaayaka), Ravana, Gaandharva, Gouri, Kashyapa, Baana, Swayambhoo, Bhujanga, Bhoja, Kinnara, Thrisari (Thripadi), Bolle (Mulla), Saraswathi, Manohari, Vichithrike, Sarathi-Gananatha, Koumara, Ravana-Hastha, Dwaari (Diviri), Sakati(Sakane), Vali, Nata-Nagarika, Kumbhike, Sara (Nara), Mallari, Varavaadi (Parivaadi) Yakulasti, Ambuja, Swara-mandala, Ghoshavathi, Oudumbari (Kaadumbura), and Thanthri-Sagara.

Naarada in Sangeetha Makaranda (of 13th Century): This has nineteen names of veenas: Kachchapi, Kubjika, Chithra, Vahanthi, Parivadini, Jaya, Ghoshavathi, Nakuli, Mahathi, Vaishnavi, Brahmi, Raavani, Roudri, Saraswathi, Sairandhri, Kinneri, Koormi and Ghoshaka.

Shri Nijaguna Yogi in Viveka-Chinthamani (of 14-15th Centuries): has given the following twenty-two names of the stringed instruments (veenas): Vipanchike, Chithra-Ghoshavali, Chithrike, Lakulasti, Koormiki, Kubjaki, Kinnari, Parivaadini, Thisathi, Thumbura, Kaasyapa, Brahma, Saaranga, Saara, Akaasha, Antharveena, Rudra-veena Anaavidhe, Raavana-Hastha, Chakana, Vallaki and Alaavini.

Some other names found are: "Vasanthi, Jyesta, Vallabhi, Jyothishmathi, Shatha-Thanthri, Thrithantri, Thanwari, Shushkala, Kapila, Madhuvanthi, Ghona, Madhuswari, Gada, Praasari, Bala-Saraswathi, Modaki, Madhusyandini, Maha, Padma, Swaraangi, Maththakokila,

Nishaanka, Anivani, Thipiri, Saakane, Valli, Naata, Sagarika, Kumbhaka, Kolashti etc!"

During Moghal's Rule: Many verieties of Persian string instruments were introduced as well as Hindusthani classical music style was developed. But these did not affect seriously the Carnatic music and its developments in the south India. Some of the above instruments were slightly altered and used in Hindusthani styles. Amir Khusro combined Indian and Persian music styles. The modifed string instruments now commonly used are; Been, Thaanpuri, Kanoon, Mayoori-veena (Persian Thaos!), Sitar, Sarod, Dilruba, Sarangi, Santhoor, Violin, Mandolin, Viola, etc. Some of these are becoming popular in south India also. It was during this period the Indian clasical music bifurcated into Carnatic system in south India and Hindustani systems in North India.

Veenas in ancient Tamil literature

Many details of classical music and veenas are available in the ancient Tamil literature, such as "Silappadikaram, Paripadala, Thivakaran" etc., of around 500-600 AC. Isai is the Tamil word for music, which includes geetha, vaadya and naatya, that is, vocal, instrumental and dance. These express the internal emotions of the artists (specially the devotion to God) in those three components of Isai. The string instrument veena was known as "yaaz (or yaal)" and its many names (varieties) are given. Eri- yaal had two types, one of two and another of 21 strings, Makara-yaal had seventeen strings, Sekatutu-yaal had 7 strings, Thumburu-yaal had nine strings, Maruth-yaal and Deva-yaal had only single strings, Naarada's Periyaal (Mahathi veena) and Saraswathi's Keechakya (Kachchapi) yaal had thousand strings to recite infinite number of raagams!

In another literary work, Kalladam of ninth century, some more names mentioned are: Seeri yaal of seven strings, Sengotti yaal of fourteen strings, Sagoda yaal of sixteen strings, Magara yaal of seventeen or

nineteen strings, Peri yaal and Vil yaal of twenty one strings etc. These authors have also described many gamaka reciting techniques, which can be applied only for veena or yaals. All these clearly indicate the popularity of veena in south India, at that time.

Gayathri (Saraswathi) veena

Many experts in Carnatic classical music, at Thanjavoor in Tamilnadu, contributed to the development of veena into the present version of Saraswathi veena. Govinda Dikshithar (father of famous Venkatamukhi), Gopala Nayak, Raghunath Nayak, the administrator of Thanjavoor and finally Thulajendra, were the main architects of the 24 frets, 4 recital and 3 laya (thaala) stringed Saraswathi veena. As there are 24 frets in number, it is also named as Gaayathri veena since the sacred Gaayathri manthra stanzas have 24 letters! The four strings are usually kept in Sadharana or madhyama shruthis. The four strings are known as, sarane for adhara (madhya) shadja, mandra panchama, mandra shadja and anu-mandra- panchamas respectively. The present Vainkas tune these four strings, accordingly. With this, it is possible to obtain notes of three and half octaves. Considering the tonal qualities of these four strings, they are, also found suitable to play or accompany Rig-veda, Yajur-veda, Saama-veda and Atharva-veda chantings, respectively.

Great poet, Kalidasa has mentioned, Manikya, Mayuri, Vallaki veenas in his famous "Shyaamala dandakam". Also in the "Navarathna maalika" verses, Kalidasa has mentioned the names of veenas five times. While praising the Goddess Para-Shakthi (Infinite Energy!), he described how skillfully She was playing the veena with Her finger-tips using all the seven notes- saptha swaras as-

"Sa, ri, ga, ma, pa, da, ni, rathaantham veena
Sankraantha kaantha hastaantham"

Sri Adi Shankaracharya has described some veenas and their importance in the attainment of spirituality. In his very popular work,

"Soundarya Lahari", there are one hundred verses. Each one produces different results when they are practiced with special rituals. It is believed that the sixty fifth verse, "Vipanchya gaayanthi...." if repeated, with special rituals and techniques for 48 days, makes the Vainika, attain the skill of veena recital techniques. He has praised Goddess in "Raja Rajeshwari Ashtaka" (8 verses), as "veena-venu-vinoda mandithakare, veerasana samsthithaa". He praised Goddess Madurai Meenakshi as "veena-venu-mridanga vaadya rasike" assuming, that Goddess considers veena as the supreme of all the best musical instruments, in the stringed, wind and percussion categories!

* * * * *

Chapter - 3

Saraswathi or Gayathri Veena

The sound veena creates in our mind, a picture of a huge wooden instrument, with a large wooden resonator attached to a long frame with wax mounted frets and strings passing over them. This is the present version of the veena which is shown in the hands of Goddess of knowledge (vidya) and music, Saraswathi. With the growth of civilization, varieties of vocal music, stringed instruments grew, while, accompanying percussion and wind instruments also improved side by side. Science and technologies helped the modifiications of these many versions of stringed, percussion and air blown wind instruments.

Many types of multi-stringed resonating instruments, with and without frets entered this field. At Thanjavoor, learned musicians like, Govinda Dikshithar, Gopala Nayak, Raghunatha Nayak and many others, also, in many other places, helped to develop the veena. It was Thulajendra,(Ref: Musicologist Parameshwara's "Veena Rahasya", critique 'Veena Lakshana Vimarshe', by Dr. Ra. Sathya Narayana in Kannada) who gave the final form for this, about three hundred years ago, as the present twenty four frets and seven stringed, a wonderful perfect musical instrument. It appears that this is the final stage of innovations, since no other changes in the basic structure and principles took place during these last three four centuries. This is an invaluable contribution to the field of classical music. Almost at the same time, Venkatamukhi (Venkatesh Dikshithar, son of Govinda Dikshithar) had another invaluable contribution to the classical music. With a strong mathematical foundation of sound, notes, and swara-sthanas, he classified the seventy two melakartha or Janaka raagas and arranged them in twelve groups or Chakras. These have again 484 sub-groups (janya- raagas). Venkatamukhi had challenged that no one can add to

or remove any raagas or swaras from this arrangement! Of course, it is possible to imagine infinite varieties of raagas outside this which are impossible to sing due to innumerable intricacies.

It is thus, that the Saraswathi veena is considered ideal for its placements of the frets with rigid mathematical formulations (in geometric progression), obeying the laws of vibrations of the stretched strings. Principles of resonance, sympathetic vibrations, harmonics, overtones, tonal qualities, etc, can be very clearly and mathematically explained using veena. In addition, it has structure and functions comparable with our body "Deivy or Gaathra veena". This, perhaps, is a very rare string instrument which has the shruthi, thaala (mother and fathers of classical music) and ability to render any raagas of Indian classical or even western music. This has most melodious, sweet tonal qualities, closest to the human voice, and ability to render exactly all the finer nuances of vocal renderings. That is why it is supreme among all the musical instruments.

Construction and functional details

Veena is usually constructed by skilled craftsmen as cottage industry in many parts of our country, like Thanjavooru of Thamilnadu, Mysore, Bangalore of Karnataka, Bobbili, near Hyderabad of Andhra Pradesh, Trivandrum of Kerala and few other places. Well aged, seasoned jack-fruit wood is very commonly used due to its sound quality, resistance to termites and suppleness which makes carving easy. Rarely rose-wood is used in Mysore. In Andhra, mango wood (easily available in plenty) is used. The quality of wood, thickness, size and shape of the resonator bowl, their designs, etc. affect the naadam or tonal qualities, accounting for small differences, in veenas built in these places. Hence they are well known by their places of fabrications, such as Thanjavoor veenas, Mysore veenas, Bobbili veenas etc.

Veena is usually constructed in three separate parts and then assembled. Very rarely, it is constructed from a single piece Ekanda veena, which is more expensive. The main parts of the veena, are a large hollow

resonator, long hollow semi-circular column of about 10-12 cm, width, and 85 to 90 cm, length, covered with a thin plank (finger-fret-board) or dandi, and artistically carved wooden head of Sharabha, Yali or lion, for ornamentation.

Resonator (Kuda)

This is a thin hollow large hemisphere of about 40-45 cm width carved in seasoned jack- wood (or rose wood) and covered with a slightly curved thin plank of jack- wood (or rarely rose wood in Mysore veena). This is slightly thicker and stronger in Thanjavooru veenas, to make it possible to get higher note vibrations, or gamakas by cross-pulling the strings to larger extent, which continuously increases the pitch (swaras) to the octaves (as in Bala Chandar's style). At the right end of this cover lid, a Naaga-pasha is fixed to bind one end of the seven strings. In the middle, wooden bridge (kudurai or ghoda in sitar!) is mounted, to which a thin sheet of brass or stainless steel plate (rekhu or pathrika) is bonded. Ivory or plastic pieces are attached on this lid, for ornamentation. During the veena recitals, the vibrations of the strings are conducted through the rekhu and bridge (ajna chakra- refer chapter... 7) into the bowl (the sahasrara- pineal glands in the brain!)and sympathetically vibrate (resonate) the volume of air in the bowl. These vibrations, overtones and the resonations of other strings combine to enrich the original vibrations, and this pleasing sweet, nada is experienced by the listeners. This naada is closest to the human voice, due to similarities of structure and functions with the human body and many other factors. This has superb, tonal qualities and purities, better than human voice. Nowadays, contact microphone pickup is attached to this board for obtaining louder sound through the amplifier systems. However the melody and tonal qualities of the sounds (naada) are to be sacrificed.

Parts of Sarawathi Veena

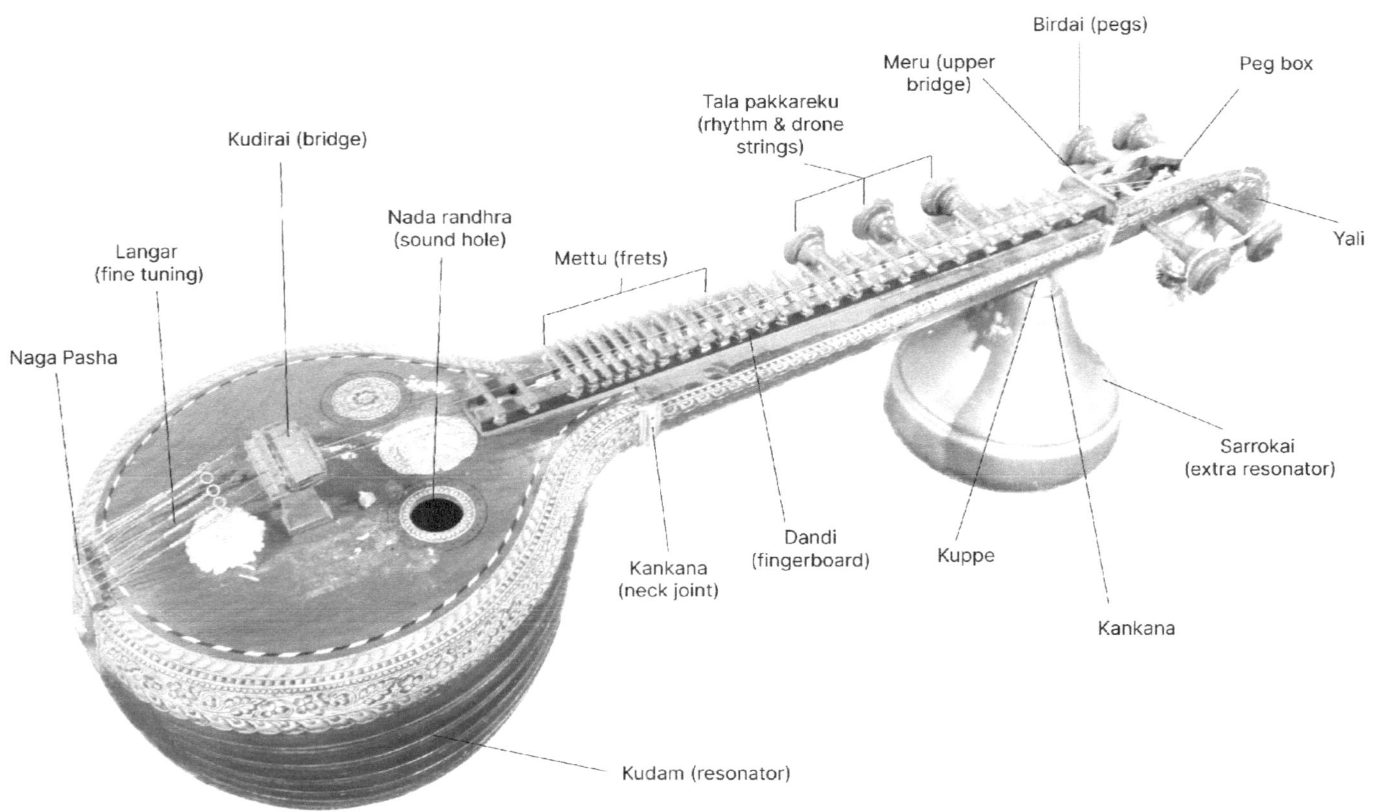

Veena dandi or finger-fret-board

Incidentally, in the Vedic period (3500-2500 B.C.), our spinal cord was named as veena dandi, even when the people had no idea of the Saraswathi veena and its close similarity with our body anatomy and physiologies! God created human body was referred as deivy or manushi veena and man-made wooden stringed instruments as daru veena.

This is a thin hollow jack-fruit wooden column of about 80-90 cm length and 10-12 cm. semicircular cross-sections, covered with a thin flat wooden plank to support the wax bonded frets (fret-board). One end of this is joined with the resonator- kuda (at kankana in the picture). The other end is connected with the artistically designed wooden head of Yali (the most powerful animal, Sharabha) or lion, for ornamentation. A supporting light kuda (of goard or fiber) is also attached to this end. Fourteen holes are made across the dandi for seven knobs (biradai) to tie the other ends of the strings for tuning i.e. to adjust the tension (shruthis).

Special wax composition, is softened, kneaded and placed along the fret board as rails (of 2 cms. height and 1 cm width). With the meru at one end, twenty four frets (rods of brass or steel each of 6.5 cm length and 4 mm diameter), are fixed on the wax rails before it completely hardens. The spaces or gaps between each frets gradually decrease from about 4-5 cm to about 4-5 mms towards the bridge. This placing is to be done very carefully and accurately at the swara sthaanas, according to the accurate mathematical principles of geometric progression of algebra. The minimum length of the vibrating segment between the bridge and the nearest fret is one fourth (¼) of the maximum length of vibration! Then the second octaves of the tuned notes can be obtained in every string!

Four strings of different gauges (29, 27, 22 and 20), or, thicknesses (0.35, 0.42, 0.71 and 0.91mms respectively), are tied with their one end to the Naaga- Paasha and the other end to the knobs at the other end of the dandi. These strings pass through the grooves on the rekhu with intimate contact and then through the grooves in the meru, at the other end. A small gap of 2 mm is left between the strings and frets. By rotating the knobs, the tension (shruthi) of the strings can be adjusted to the desired pitch. The first two strings, sarane (adhara shadja) and the mandra panchama are made up of steel, the third and fourth, mandra shadja and the anu-mandra panchama, respectively, are of brass or copper. Sometimes, these two are also of steel, over which, very thin copper strands are wound. These twisted strings are said to produce better tonal qualities.

When these strings are plucked near the bridge, they can produce vibrations of any desired frequencies or sound of any pitch. Vainikas adjust the tensions (shruthi) according to their conveniences of rendering the concert. When the entire length of the string vibrates, the sarane should produce the adhara shadja (sa). In common or sadharana shruthi - technique, the second string should be in mandra panchama (half of pa), third string in mandra shadja (half of sa.) and the fourth in anu-mandra panchama (quarter of pa).

By pressing the sarane strings, when different frets are contacted one by one, the length of vibrating segments decrease and their frequencies increase, producing the first octaves i.e., thaara shadja, (400) at the 12th fret and athi--thaara shadja (800) at the last 24th fret.. The positions of the frets are very carefully adjusted to give tnote positions, swara sthanas, of two prakrithi swaras (madhya sthaayee sa at meru, and pa) and five vikrithi swaras (ni, ga, ma, dha, ni) up to the octave ie. Thaara sthaayee, sa. in the twelfth fret. When the 24th fret is contacted, the notes obtained by these four strings are, athi-thaara shadja, thaara panchama, thaara shadja, and madhya panchama respectively. It is possible to obtain three and half octaves of the notes by tuning in sadharana shruthis.

Three stainless steel tempered strings of 29, 29 (same as the sarane string) and 32 gauges, pass from the naaga-paasha, contacting the

side rekhu, through the sides of the dandi, and are tied to the three knobs. Their tensions or shruthis can be adjusted to madhya-shadja, madhya-panchama and thaara- shadja, respectively. These were known as shruthi strings earlier. Vainikas are now using them to show the rhythm or thaala, by plucking with little finger and these are now called as thaala strings.

This is the structure of Saraswathi veena innovated by Govinda Dikshithar, Gopala Nayak and Raghunatha Nayak of Thanjavooru and finally Thulajendra. (But some do not mention Thulajendra's name). Many surprising useful information and its supremacy are described in the later chapters.

The famous stringed instrument, now called as sitar, is only a modified earlier form of Eka raaga swara mela veena, in which, the positions of the frets are to be changed for different raagas. This has many similarities, in the structure, plucking and rendering techniques, etc, with veena. Dr. R.K. Soorya Narayana a well known Vainaka has told that veena is the mother of sitar.

Recent modifications

Some veena manufacturing concerns, innovative Vainikas and scientists have thought of resolving inconveniences and drawbacks of this huge structure. They have tried to apply the modern technologies, according to the present requirements. But the basic structure of twenty four frets, seven strings, length y fret board, and large size of resonator, could not be changed without sacrificing quality of tones.. It is scientifically proved fact, when the sizes of the resonators or the lengths of the vibrating strings are reduced below certain limits, the tonal qualities and bass- richness of the sound become poor.

Following are some of the changes made so far

1. Easily breakable thin wooden resonator and support structures are replaced by unbreakable fiber structures.

2. Wax structure, very often gets softened and the frets get displaced in hot summers. The repositioning of the frets is quite expensive and highly skilled persons are required for this sensitive mela (or swara- sthaana) settings. The frets are fixed by using the nuts and bolts- system which can be moved along the two metal strips (rails) on the dandi. The Vainikas can themselves adjust them easily in the required exact positions.

3. To listen the very fine and weak resonating sounds, gamakas and overtones, etc, sensors, contact microphones or electromagnetic pickups (in which case all the strings should be magnetic) are used and connected to the amplifier systems. Nowadays, loud music is required to reach the audience who number in hundreds, and delicacies are slightly sacrificed for volume.

4. The wooden resonator and the support are replaced by detachable structures. In these, one contains a small amplifier and the other, an adjustable shruthi box. This detachable veena is easier to do packing, and carry to the place of concert. This also has an advantage in the concerts, where the Vainika can listen to what he is rendering even if the monitoring speakers are not provided.

5. Some are also trying to incorporate the modern software technology, as in key-boards, rhythm-pads, etc. This electronic veena. can be used for rendering sounds of veena, flute, violin, mandolin, saxophone, etc!

Many aristocratic Vainikas still do not accept this modification for used in the concerts. According to them, these do not have the enriched tonal qualities of the convensional veena, as this does not have the very essential wooden resonator in it. It is like a man, without pineal glands (Sahasrara!). But most of the present audience do not value much, the sweetness, melody and good tonal qualities, but like loud exciting sound and fast rendering techniques.

All these modifications with the applications of the modern technology and facilities have created curiosity and attract the audience.

These modifications have made learning and rendering of veena, much easier and attract the younger generation to pursue studying veena.

At present I am also thinking seriously, about some modifications which can retain the original tonal qualities of the wooden Saraswathi veenas by retaining the wooden resonator. I have been successful in using the adjustable frets along the metal rails, without using wax. It is easily possible to incorporate a shruthi box or a small amplifier in the support kuda or they can be used separately. Contact sound pickups also can be used near the bridge. Naada- randhra or sound-hole is made on the lid of the resonator to enrich the naada. As the shruthi adjusting wooden pegs (birades) frequently slips during concerts, metallic keys are more suitable instead. All these changes made is found to improve the tonal qualities almost close to the conventional veena as the large sized resonator is retained. I have named it **"Aruna-akshi Veena"** as propagation of veena is my vision!

* * * * *

Chapter - 4

Science of Saraswathi Veena

Classical music and verities of musical instruments developed in India side by side complimentary to each other, since a very long time even before the Vedic period. The advances in science and technologies have their lion's share in these innovations. The most valuable contributions to these fields are, the development of the perfect musical instrument veena, and the classification of the 72 melakartha janaka ragas (and many janya ragas), as well as, grouping them in twelve chakras by Venkatamukhi, in the eighteenth century. No one can deny the fact that the God created structure and functioning of the various parts our body and organs are the most complicated ones in this world. Even now, we are unable to understand and explain the secrets of the methods of controlling all the functions of our bodies by the brain. This, God's creation "gaathra veena" is a perfect living being and has many similarities, with the man created wooden "daaru veena" which is also a perfect musical instrument. Some of the scientific aspects discussed briefly are connected with: anatomy (body structure), physiology (body functions), and physics (vibrations, waves, harmonics, overtones, acoustics and naada), hearing and analysis of sounds through ears, tuning techniques, types of melas and shruthis etc. Spiritual aspects, Naada- Yoga is dealt separately in chapters seven.

Veena and human anatomy

Our spine (spinal cord) has been surprisingly mentioned as "veena dandi" in the Vedas, Upanishaths etc. This spinal cord extends from the pelvis region to the (cerebral) brain region. Normally it contains twenty four vertebrae, out of which the lower five are named as lumbar, middle twelve are thoraisic (dorsal), and the top seven are cervical, according

to the modern anatomy. In veena, the finger-board carries twenty four frets and the strings extend from the meru to the bridge. The first five steps (frets) refer to the low pitch (mandra sthaayee notes: pa, da1, da2, ni2, ni3,), the middle twelve frets refer to middle pitch (madhya sthayee notes: sa, ri1, ri2, ga2, ga3, ma1, ma2, pa, da1, da2, ni2, ni3,) and the seven steps at the other end refer to the high pitch thaara sthaayee notes: sa, ri1, ri2, ga2, ga3, ma1, ma2,), while playing the veena in the second-mandra panchama string! (refer: chapter 7;- Naada-Yoga). The sizes of the vertebrae and spaces in between, gradually decrease from the lumbar to the cervical region. Similarly, the spaces between the frets decreases mathematically from the meru to the other end. The length of the spinal cord is around thirty five inches (nearly half of the height of a normal person). The lengths of strings or the distance between the meru of veena (mooladhara chakra, in human body at the pelvis,) and the bridge (ajna- chakra between the eye brows, according to the yogic sciences,) is also approximately the same! These seven strings of the man made daru veena, are the saptha- naadis of the God made gaathra veena (in the spiritual-Yogic science), which also resemble the nerve-systems in the spinal cord! The Yaali (Lions- Sharaba) head can compared to the sacrum of spine support of the human body.

Veena and Physiology

Millions of nerve cells and nerves carry the various stimulations created at the different parts of the body by sensory organs, through the spinal cord to the brain. The most surprising and yet unexplained part played by the brain is, how it exactly analyses, differentiates and stores these micro-micro signal energies and interprets them in the form of personal experiences through our five sensory organs (panchaiendriyas), namely the ears (sound), vision (eyes), taste (tongue), fragrance (nose), contact and hotness (skin)!

It is not possible to explain these experiences by any words, languages or signs, unless others have similar experiences! This also applies to, how the brain controls the respiratory system, blood circulatory systems, various glands etc, and also many other activities of the different parts of our body. In veena the plucking causes vibrations of the strings. This energy moves back and forth between meru and the bridge. This energy causes similar vibrations in the air medium in contact, and also conducted through the bridge to the air in the resonator and produces the complex vibrations in it. All these vibration energies combine together, travel, get collected by the ears and finally reach the brain which interprets their pitch, volume and timbre or the quality of sound, and also differentiates them (naada and naada-bheda).

Acoustics

Vibrations produced by plucking or bowing the strings, blowing the wind instruments and striking the percussion instruments, create similar vibration energies in the medium (air, gases, liquids, or solids) in contact with them. These have their characteristic properties, frequency (number of vibrations per second), amplitude (energy) of vibrations, and the complexity of wave-forms result in tone differences (pitch, loudness, and timbre or qualities). Transverse vibration-waves produced by the instruments "aahatha naada" travel in air as longitudinal waves with certain velocity, v (about 333 meters/second which is different at different temperatures and the travelling media like solids, liquids, or gases). The wave length (λ) is inversely proportional to its frequency (n). These are equated as: Velocity= frequency × wave-length, i.e. $v = n\lambda = 333$ m/sec, in air at 0°C in air medium, and increases with temperature. Sound travels as longitudinal pressure waves inany medium but not in vaccum.

The intensity of sound is a subjective experience of listening of a person. The intensity of sound energy I, is measured by comparing this with threshold sound energy I_0 which can be just heard. It is expressed as the ratio of intensity of sound heard, to his threshold intensity of listening, i.e. I/I_0 in the logarithmic scale to the base 10. For example when the sound energies are 10, 100, 1,000, or 10,000,

times the threshold level of just listening, they are given by the values 1, 2, 3, 4, Bells, or 10, 20, 30, 40, deci-Bells (dB).

The ear has mainly three parts, the outer, middle and the inner. The pinna of the outer ear collects the longitudinal sound waves reaching it through air and transmits through the auditory canal, to the ear-drum (tympanic membrane). The middle ear is an air filled cavity containing three very small bones, shaped as hammer (malleus), anvil (incus) and stirrup (stapes), which are linked together. These connect the membrane to the oval window of the inner ear. Sound energy waves received are amplified in the middle ear. The inner ear contains semi fluid structure, cochlea. When the cochlea is stretched, its length becomes about 30 mms in which about 20,000 micro-fine hair cells of fiber like nerve structures of different lengths (reeds) can be found in this basilar membrane. The sound (pressure) wave energy entering, stimulates particular group of these basilar reeds by resonance with frequencies ranging from about 25 to 20,000 Hertz. These nerve signals pass through the auditory nerves and reach the brain. The brain analyzes interprets and creates the "feeling or the experience" of the pitch, volume, the quality or timbre of the sound (naada) and also, the minute differences (naada bedha) in the sounds received by the listener. These "feelings or personal experiences" cannot be explained by any words. One has to experience them by himself, like the sages experiencing the effects of their meditations and the eternal bliss, which they also cannot explain to others!

Physics of veena playing techniques

Plucking of any strings of veena under tension (T), makes them to vibrate between the bridge and the fret contacted by pressing the string, forming one half sinusoidal waves. The length of the vibrating segment (l) is equal to half of the wave-length (λ) of the fundamental mode of vibration. The frequency (n) of the vibrations is the number of vibrations/second, which is the fundamental frequency (n) of the first harmonic. The amplitude is the maximum displacement of the particle in the middle of the string (anti-node). The energy of vibration is proportional to the squares of their frequencies and amplitudes.

According to the laws of vibrations of the stretched strings, the frequency of vibrations, (n), is inversely proportional to the length of the vibrating segments,(l), thickness (or diameter, d) of the strings (or square root of its mass/unit length, (m), and directly proportional to the square root of the tension (T) when the other factors are kept constant. These are related by the formula, $\frac{1}{2l}\left(\frac{T}{M}\right)^{1/2}$. All these three laws of vibrations are to be followed by the Vainikas (or any stringed instrument players) in whatever techniques (banis), they play!

The first law

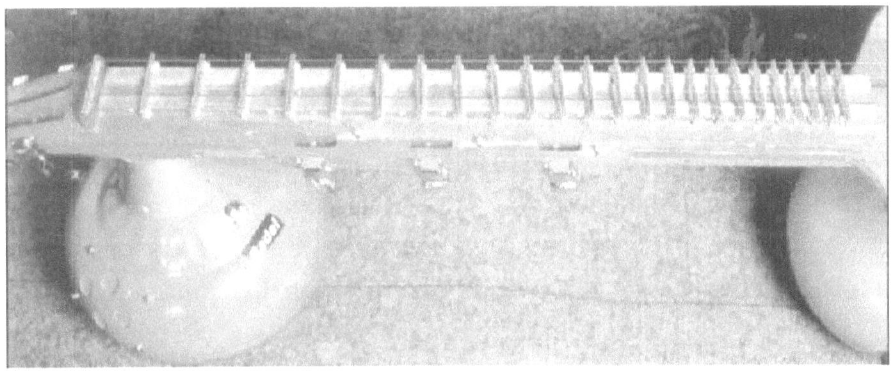

Veena 24 mansions - Sarikas on fret board in geometric progression

According to this, the frequency of the fundamental note, n, is inversely proportional to the length of the vibrating segment, l, i.e. n.l = a constant. In other words, the frequency becomes double, 2n, when the length is reduced to half. The 24 frets are very accurately spaced and fixed in the mathematica geometrical progression with respect to the meru, so that the 24 spaces (mansions) formed between them, gradually decrease from the meru towards the bridge. This helps the Vainika to play any notes as required by contacting the frets with the strings. The frequencies of say, the madhyama

sthayee notes, n = sa, ri_1, ri_2, ga_2, ga_3 etc, increase towards the bridge and become double = its first octave = 2n = thaara sthayee notes, sa, ri_1, ri_2, ga_2, ga_3, etc, when the length decreases to half. Ahobila in his "Sangeetha Vaangmaya" and Dr. Nookala Chinna Sathya Narayana, in his "Sangeetha Shasthra Sudharnava" have explained this law as "when the frequency increases, the length decreases and the swara sthaanas are located according to the length of the strings, the thaara shadjam is in the middle of the string, and the madhyama is in the middle of two shadjas!"

The second law

According to this, the frequency of vibration is inversely proportional to the square root of the mass/unit length of the strings, or the thickness (diameter) for the same material. That is, the frequencies of the madhyama sthayees notes n=sa, ri_1, ri_2, ga_2, ga_3, etc, become double, its first octave=2n=thara sthayees notes, sa, ri_1, ri_2, ga_2, ga_3, etc, when a string of half thickness is used. In veena, four strings of different thicknesses (gauges) are used to obtain wider ranges of frequencies and higher octaves. Usually the saarane or shadja has thickness, 0.35mms (29 gauge), mandra panchama has, 0.42 mms (27 gauge), mandra shadja has 0.71 mms (22 gauge) and anu-mandra panchama has 0.91 mms. (20 gauge). In the commonly used "saadharana shruthi" tuning method, the tensions are adjusted, without contacting the strings, as: aadhara shadja-the most suitable frequency (say, sa, 200), in the first string sarane, then mandra shadja becomes half of sa (100) in the third string. Similarly the mandra panchama (pa) in the second string becomes its half, pa/2, in the anu-mandra panchama in the fourth string. When the last frets are contacted with the strings by touching with the finger, the lengths become shortest (1/4th) and the frequencies become four times, or the second octaves, of the corresponding swaras, or frequencies. With this, it is possible to get about three and half octaves in veena. Both these laws hold good only when the tensions are kept constant i.e. "without altering the shuthi". Applying these two laws, Vainikas can play the veena with

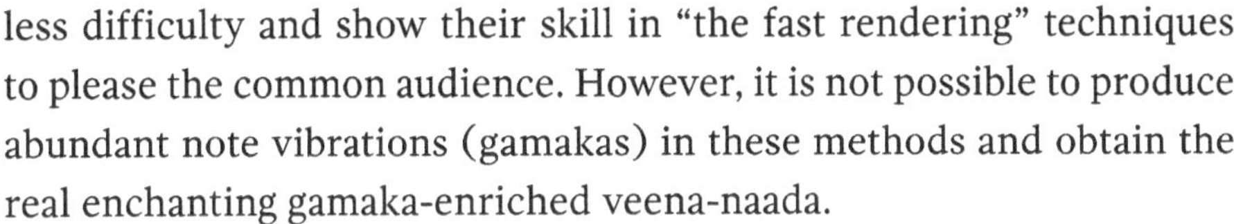

less difficulty and show their skill in "the fast rendering" techniques to please the common audience. However, it is not possible to produce abundant note vibrations (gamakas) in these methods and obtain the real enchanting gamaka-enriched veena-naada.

The third law

This states that, the frequency of vibration of a string of definite length is directly proportional to the square root of its stretching tension (T). Accordingly the fundamental frequencies of vibrations say, n, madhya sthaayees notes, sa, ri_1, ri_2, ga_2, ga_3.....etc, become, double, its octave, 2n=thaara sthaayee notes, sa, ri_1, ri_2, ga_2, ga_3.....etc, when the tension is increased four times. During the concert, the Vainikas, without lifting the fingers from the particular fret, stretch (pull) the plucked string across and vibrate or shake it with the same fingers to produce continuous note-vibrations or gamakas. This can be incorporated to any notes. This technique requires intensive practice. While vibrating the strings the tension increases and accordingly the frequency of the notes continuously increase to the higher ones and even to the higher octaves (Bala Chander's style!). This can be represented, as: sa-ri_1-ri_2-ga_2-ga_3 etc,) to any higher notes. Since there are no discontinuities, infinite verities of raagas can be imagined! Combining this third law with the first and the second laws of vibrations an expert Vainika can expose his mano- dharma (Saathvic feelings or divine bhaava) and can induce similar rasa or bhaava with the listeners. All these laws of vibrations of the stretched strings apply in general to all the stringed instruments!

Resonance: Sympathetic Vibrations

Sometimes a number of extra strings are stretched under the rendering strings in the string instruments. These are tuned to some desired frequencies for enrichment of the sound. Two strings of same material, same length, and stretched under same tensions have equal natural frequencies of vibrations. When one of the strings is vibrated by

plucking the energy is conducted through the medium, and makes the other to vibrate with the same frequency! This is known as resonance which causes sympathetic vibrations. These extra strings vibrate sympathetically when suitably tuned, producing enrichment of sound, naada. Sitar and some string musical instruments (very rarely in veena) use, fifteen to about twenty sympathetically vibrating strings.

Voice and Voice- Differences (Naada and Naada Bheda)

When a string, stretched between two points is plucked, it vibrates simple harmonically, forming nodes at the fixed points and anti-node in between, with maximum displacement = amplitude, A. This is its first harmonic of fundamental frequency = n. This lowest frequency in the sarane string, is adjusted by the musician to his suitability and is the adhara shadja (or the Shruthi).

The instantaneous displacement of any particle in the string (or medium) is represented mathematically. For this simple harmonic motion (SHM.), it is given by, $x = a.Sine2\pi nt$,... (Eqs....4-1), where, **a**, is the amplitude (maximum displacement) and **t**, is the time elapsed. The energy of this vibration, $E = 2\pi^2 n^2 a^2 m$, where m is the mass of vibrating string. Along with this, fundamental mode of vibration, string can also vibrate in the second, third, fourth, etc, harmonics with the amplitudes a_1, a_2, a_3, etc, and with the corresponding frequencies, 2n, 3n, 4n, etc, with their nodes at the ends figure (4-1, 2, 3, 4, 5, etc.).

$x_1 = a_1 Sin\ 2\pi(2nt)$,...... (4.2),
$x_2 = a_2\ Sin\ 2\pi(3nt)$,....... (4.3)
$x_3 = a_3\ Sin\ 2\pi(4nt)$,.......... (4.4) etc.

These are the first, second third, etc., over tones of frequencies, twice, thrice, four times etc. However the vibration energies e_1, e_2, e_3, e_4 etc, of overtones are quite small, but different in different cases. These instantaneous displacements with corresponding energies, algebraically, add up together to have resultant instantaneous displacement, $X = x + x_1 + x_2 + x_3$....... etc. Their energies are proportional to the product of squares of frequencies (n2), and squares of amplitudes (a2), forming resultant wave-forms of fundamental notes. These merging components are different for different persons and also different for vibrating string instruments, air columns, membranes etc, because of the minute structural differences! In addition, the energies of sympathetic vibrations also merge with the energies of fundamental notes. All these cause the voice differences or naada-bheda even when

1 to 5 Harmonics of vibrating strings

the fundamental frequencies or shruthis, are same. In other words, when many people sing (or instruments are played) together, even with the same shruthi or pitch, the listeners will not have any difficulties of distinguishing or identifications! The resultant wave forms (diagrams A and B are for male deep bass note and C, female treble note and their differences are very accurately analyzed by our brain as sound (naada) and differentiated as naada-bedha. Our brains are capible of differentiating them very accurately. Mathematically, these wave-forms can be represented by Fourier series. By converting it to digital presentation the naada and naada bheda can be analyzed by using Fast

Fourier Transform (FFT) techniques. By this, the components of the harmonics in various gamakas, shruthis and raagas can be found (refer- Chapter 11).

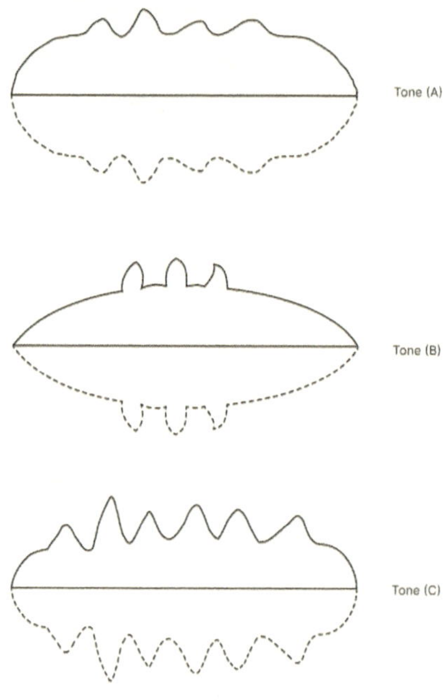

Voice Difference

Late Prof. G.T. Narayana Rao (of Mysore), a well-known critic of fine arts and music as well as writer on modern science, astronomy etc, wrote in one of his published articles, in appreciation of the veena naada as follows:

"The main basic qualities of purity of tone, deep sonorous overtones, gliding tremulous gamakas, reverberating bewitchingly charming undertones, are superb and closest to human whispers and hummings. The swara-raaga-gathi oriented veena rendering, makes the listener caught in the web of pleasant jingling notes. The raaga-bhaava-krithi oriented method of rendering (presentation) makes the listeners' thoughts, reach and cross the lofty heights of art experience leading to the rasa-samaadhi!"

Late, Prof. G T Narayana Rao. a wellknown musicologist and Professor of Mathematics, had visited me at our residence at Mangalore, on one fine evening and listened enthusiastically, my technique of veena rendering and classical music enriched by gamakas (as taught me by Sri Ananthapadmanabhan of Thrissur), for about four hours! He appreciated my interest, constant practice and devotion to music, and encouraged me to proceed in this path. He had organized a veena concert at the reputed Veene Sheshanna Bhavana at Mysore on 28th June 2008. He had introduced me in the Weekly, "Mysore Star" on 26th June. When we reached Mysore on 28th morning, shocking news of his sad demise, just on the previous night by heart attack, was waiting for us.

Swara-Mela structures of veenas

Fixing the frets at the different positions on the fret-board, to match the various notes produced while plucking the strings is known as mela setting. Rama Amaathya of Andhra, had mentioned the name, Rudra veena (as Shiva was the first inventor of veena), and described the setting of the positions of the frets for obtaining the different notes (swara-sthanas), in his famous work **"Swara-Mela-Kalanidhi"**. According to this, the three varieties of veenas of different mela settings are:

1. Shuddha - swara-mela-veena,
2. Madhya - swara-mela-veena,
3. Achutha Rajendra (or Raghu Nathendra) swara-mela-veena,

In each system, there are two varieties

a. **Eka raaga-swara-mela-veena:** In this the fret- positions are fixed according to the notes of a particular raaga, as in the case of sitar. For rendering other raagas, new arrangements of frets are to be done.

b. **Sarva raaga-swara-mela veena:** In this method, the frets are positioned at definite places according to all the swara sthaanas of music. Hence any raaga can be rendered without changing the fret positions.

Venkata Mukhi in his famous published work "Chathurdandi Prakashike" meaning, "four pillars of Carnatic classical music", has devoted one complete chapter for the detailed description of veena and its importance only. He has named the thaala strings as, "Jhallika (madhya shadja), madhya panchama, and Teepi (thaara shadja)"respectively.

Eka-thanthrika veena: Venkata Mukhi had indicated that, by using only one string, it is possible to obtain three octaves by slightly increasing the length of the string. But it is not possible for a normal person to stretch both hands to that extend easily! (Note: Detailed descriptions and explanations of the above are out of scope of this book, since the structures and the numbers of frets in the veenas at that time, were different, and none of the above methods are used nowadays after the entry of the Saraswathi veena.)

Saraswathy veena tuning methods

Vainikas, commonly tune the strings and set the veena strings in the sadharana shruthi and sometimes in the madhyama shruthis. This twenty four frets, seven strings, Saraswathy veena is sarva raaga mela veena.

Sadharana (commonly used) shruthi

When the string is vibrating with its full length that is without contacting any frets it forms its first harmonic of fundamental note of the lowest frequency (n). Tuning the strings in this condition is setting of shruthi. The note adjusted to the most convenience of the Vainika in this first string, saarane, is the aadhara shadja, say, madhya sthaayee, sa. The other three strings are then tuned to mandra panchama, pa, mandra shadja, sa and anu- mandra panchama, pa, respectively. With this tuning, when the last twenty fourth fret is contacted by the strings, lengths of the segments up to the bridge, reduce to minimum i.e. one fourth(1/) When plucked, they vibrate with maximum frequencies, four times of the notes, athi-thaara-shadja, thaara-panchama, thaara-shadja, and madhya-panchamas, respectively. While plucking, if the frets under the first saarane string are contacted one by one, the notes we get are: madhya sthayee-(sa), ri_1, ri_2, ga_2, ga_3, ma_1, ma_2, pa, dha_1, dha_2, ni_2, ni_3, and thaara sthayee- sa, ri_1, ri_2, ga_2, ga_3, ma_1, ma_2, Pa, dha_1, dha_2, ni_2, ni_3, and athi-thaara-sthaayee-sa, in the last twenty fourth, fret are obtained. This makes it possible to obtain three and half octaves while rendering veena

Madhyama shruthi

Some raagas ending in nishadha, dhaivatha and panchamas, if rendered in the sadharana shruthi, do not become attractive. In such cases, musicians render in the madhyama shruthi. When the veena strings are tuned in the madhyama shruthi, the notes (swara-sthanas) produced at the meru are mandra-panchama, mandra- shadja, anu-mandra-panchama, and anu- mandra- shadjas, in the sarane and the other three strings respectively. Similarly, in the last fret, the available notes (swara-sthaanas) are: thaara-panchama, thaara-shadja, and madhya-panchama and madhya shadjas respectively. However this method is rather theoretical only, and not used in practice. Some Vainikas consider first string sarane as mandra panchama and the third string as anu-mandra panchama and change the thaala –shruthi from sa, pa, and (thaara) sa, to sa, ma, (thaara) sa, respectively, "i.e. the middle string from pa to ma" In both the cases, while rendering the 72 mela-kartha raagas, sometimes, ri_2 becomes ga_1, ga_2 becomes ri_3, dha_2 becomes ni_1, and ni_2 becomes dha_3.

Swara-Sthaana-shifting special technique

Sometimes, during the concerts, Vainikas have to change the rendering shruthis, especially when veena is used for accompaniments. They can do it by turning the different knobs which requires few minutes in between. Now some Vainakas use a special technique known as "swara-sthaana-shifting method". This is possible as the frets are positioned in geometric progression. This note or swara sthaana shifting technique is frequently used by expert Vainikas even for longer time, unlike the

griha-bheda technic in other instruments or vocal music! The following simple explanation can be easily digested.

Vainikas tune the strings in the sadharana shruthi to his most convenient adhara shadja, sa, say, 2, shruthi, as usual. Now the swara sthaanas in saarane are: sa (in meru), ri_1, ri_2, ga_2, ga_3, ma_1, ma_2, etc. To get higher 2½, shruthi, Vainika has to play starting from the first fret as sa instead of ri_1. Now the next swara-sthaanas shift to the next positions. Similarly to get 3- shruthi, second fret is to be contacted and rendered as sa, instead of ri_2. The note positions shift further, to the next step! The Vainikas should have adequate rendering experience to venture this technique as there is a danger of confusion of swara sthaanas. This technique, which is quite different than the griha-bheda technique, cannot be explained so much clearly as in veena, with any other instruments or in vocal music. Hence it is the best perfect scientific musical instrument!

* * * * *

Chapter - 5

Veena Rendering Methods and Styles

Most of the classical music concerts and veena renderings are done, with scripts or saahithya, about praying the Lord, expressing their devotion, faith and complete surrender. Lakhs of scripts written by many pious musicians, and great persons, like, Thyagaraja, Muthuswamy Dikshithar, Shyama Shasthry, Purandara Dasa, Basavanna, Allama Prabhu, Akka Mahadevi, and many such others, have explained the spiritual aspects of the philosophy of life, in very simple words. These help the common man to digest the complicated principles of duties and goals of life, described in the Vedas and Upanishads. The expert vocalists and Vainikas render these scripts to express their devotion with emotions (bhaava) in suitable raagas. These induce similar bhaava and rasa in the pious listeners' minds and make them lost in the web of jingling music in the ocean of bliss (or aananda saagara!), which is sometimes called as bhaava or rasa Samaadhi!

Earlier, at the time of Mysore Veene Sheshanna (1852- 1926), Vainikas used to render veena, holding it vertically. Many stone sculptures of

idols of veena players in the old temples built by Hoysalas, Cholas and others, in south India, depict these. At the time of music trinities (around 1800 A.C) veena rendering was done in this manner, just like holding the thamboora or sitar vertically. However, latter and at present, the practice is to keep the veena horizontally on the lap. This helps the Vainikas as they need not worry about its instability and weight while rendering.

Before learning veena rendering, the students should have clear idea of its complicated structure and all the information, at least, given in this book. Then only the students will appreciate this heavenly music instrument veena and be proud to become good Vainikas!

Initially, students should practice the various techniques of plucking (meetus), of all the four strings with the index and middle fingers, and the three shruthi or thaala strings, with the small finger. Next they should learn the methods of tuning that is, adjusting the adhara shadja to their most convenient shruthis, two, two and half, three, four, etc. Then other strings are to be tuned usually in sadharana shruthis that is, mandra panchama, mandra shadja and anu-mandra panchamas. Similarly, the three thaala strings are tuned to madhya shadja, madhya panchamam and thaara shadjas. To experience the real bliss of sonorous overtones, reverberating undertones enriched by the delicate gamakas, Vainikas render in the lower shruthis, two or two and half. However to satiisfy the requirements and demands of the present audience, some Vainikas render in the higher, three or four shruthis with fast movements of left hand fingers and plucking of the thaala strings more often.

For veena rendering, first of all, the tuning of all the strings must be done perfectly. Any minute differences, result in apa- swaras, and very badly affect the concerts. Secondly, a clear understanding and locating the exact positions of all the swara sthaanas (notes) quickly and automatically by the left hand fingering, is to be mastered. When, various plucking techniques, gamaka technics, their incorporation in junti-varasas, are mastered, one becomes an expert Vainika. To achieve this, one should have sustained practice and adoration of veena.

Paarshwa Deva, in his, "Sangeetha Saara" has stated the requirements of ideal Vainikas, as:

"Jithendriaha pragalbhascha, sthirasana parigrahah|
Sharira soushtavopethah, karayor vijitha samaha |
Saavadhano bhayathyaktho raaga raaganga thathwavith|
Geetha vaadana dakshaschah Vainakah kaththithovaraha||"

"Excellency in veena rendering can be achieved with full control over the senses, maturity, straight sitting posture, good health, strong fingers, careful and fearless rendering, and very good knowledge of raagas, raagangas (their structural components) veena rendering and vocal music!"

Compared to all other verities of musical instruments, veena has most complicated rendering techniques. To master this, one should exert maximum efforts. Apart from these, since this is a divine instrument, spiritual practices, prayers, yogasanas, meditations on this incarnation of Goddess Saraswathi, will help to achieve good skill.

Veena rendering styles (Baanis)

There are many veena rendering styles known as baanis. These are identified by the gaayaki (singing), vaadaki (instrumental) or combined styles. In addition, methods of plucking, usage of thaala strings, skill and speed of movements in using the left hand fingers while rendering, incorporation of gamakas, raaga bhaava, saahithya bhaavas, etc. are to be considered. Differences in the styles of teaching by their teachers, structure of veenas, regional languages, types of audience, expectations of their fosters like organizers, patronizing kings in whose courts they are recognized, etc, are the main reasons for these variations. For example, Mysore rulers patronized veene Sheshanna's style, now known as Mysore bani, Thanjavoor Nayaks helped Vainikas to

develop the gamaka-rich gaayaki (vocal-singing) style or Thanjavoor bani, Kings of Vijaya Nagar Empire helped Vainikas to develop the vaadaki (instrumental rendering) style, sometimes known as Bobbili or Hyderabad or Andhra baani, the rulers of Travancore assisted their Vainikas to have their own Kerala style. Many individuals developed their own techniques, known by their names, like Bala Chandar's bani, Karaikudi brothers' bani, Emani Shankar Shasthri'style, Veenai Dhanammal's bani, Trichur Ananthapadmanabhan's combined styles, etc. At that time, there were no facilities of easy communication, recording these styles, quick travelling to other distant places, etc. There was no chance of diffusing these styles to other distant places. That is why; different baanis were confined to their own regions. Now the conditions have been changed. Many Vainikas are combining the good aspects of all other styles and use their own baanis. For example, Thrissur Anantha Padmanabhan uses such an improvised baani, which attracts the aristocratic audience, the public, as well as the younger generation-students. His son, Anand Kaushik, is also following almost same style. Such modifications and involvements of many types of accompanying modern instruments, have secured veena, international recognition and popularity.

Vainikas chose suitable raagas and styles to express their bhaava and rasa, arising in their mind, to create similar bhaava and rasas in the minds of the listeners which make them lost in the ocean of bliss or ananda!

The listeners usually identify these different styles by:

- Planning of rendering the concerts,
- Gaayaki, vaadaki or mixture of these styles,
- Abundance of usage of gamakas,
- Plucking frequencies and techniques,
- Importance given to thaalas,
- Raaga bhaava and Saahithya bhaavas,
- Richness of tonal qualities (Naada-maadhurya)

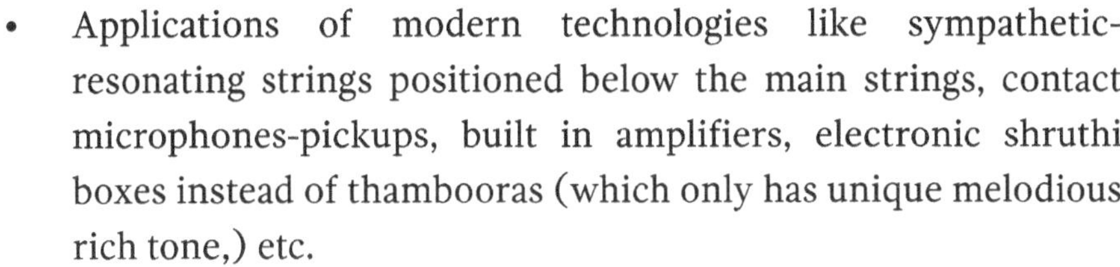

- Applications of modern technologies like sympathetic-resonating strings positioned below the main strings, contact microphones-pickups, built in amplifiers, electronic shruthi boxes instead of thambooras (which only has unique melodious rich tone,) etc.

Basic or in-depth knowledge of these various styles helps the music lovers to identify, appreciate and get involved in the classical music concerts better.

Mysore Bani (style)

The Mysore veenas have thin top cover board made up of rose-wood to get richer naada. While applying the gamakas, the strings are to be pulled laterally. This large force acting on the bridge pushes the cover board downwards, which makes the pulled strings touch the next frets. Hence, gamakas applied can have a limited short-range of 2 or 3 higher notes. This structure of cover-board and the gap between the frets and strings are slightly different in Thanjavoor veenas. This Mysore baani has the following characteristics:

- Enriched tonal quality by many short- range gamakas
- Good tonal clarity with more treble and higher volume of sound.
- Mostly split fingering techniques are used.
- Use of the finger nails for plucking
- Frequent plucking in between sahithya swaras
- Good speed in moving the left hand fingers very skillfully.

Vainika Shikhamani, Mysore Veene Sheshanna had promoted this style which has become famous as Mysore baani. Many Kings of Mysore state, were themselves, veena artists and musicians and admirers of classical vocal music, veena, violin, flute, etc instrumental renderings. They patronized many artists. Veene Sambayya, Bhairavi Naranappa, Venkatagiriappa, Veene Subbanna, Veene Shivaramayya, Veene Shamanna, Bhakshi Chikka Ramappa, Dodda Sheshanna, Shankaranarayana Rao, Sheshagiri Rao, Raja Rao, Bidaram Krishnappa,

violinist Piteel Choudayya, Devendrappa, Mysore Sadashiva Rao, Mysore Vasudeva Achar, and many others.

Thanjavoor Baani

This gaayaki (vocal-singing) style is very popular in south India. It has been contributed by many veena artists and encouraged by the rulers of Thanjavooru, since two or three centuries. This is very much enriched and ornamented by the different types of thaanams and gamaka techniques. In fact, the complicated structure of veena is most suitable for rendering in these styles. The Thanjavoor veenas have some special constructional features, suitable for rendering in these baani. While cross-pulling and vibrating the strings to larger extent to create gamakas of higher pitch variations, greater forces will act on the bridge. This can push the top cover downwards, making the strings touch the adjacent frets. But these veenas have thicker (stronger) top cover, prepared with jack-fruit tree wood, to resist these large deforming forces. This enables the Vainikas to cross- pull the strings to larger extents. By this, continuous changes in the notes can be achieved even up to their octaves! It is possible to incorporate easily any types of gamakas to any raagas. In this gaayaki style, every aspect of enriching the vocal concerts can be exactly and more beautifully presented. Sri Shankarachaarya in the sixty fifth verse of his "Soundarya Lahari" in praise of Supreme Mother, has stated as "Vipanchya gaayanthi", which means that Goddes, Lalitha Devi was rendering Her veena in the gaayaki style, as if she is singing! Goddes Saraswthi, hid Her famous veena in her sari, "Vinirbhasthitha Kachchapi,"while listening the most melodious sweetest veena voice of Goddess Lalitha as described in "Lalitha Sahasra Naamam."

Karaikkudi – Thanjavooru Baani. These modifications of Thanjavooru style is done by Subbarama and Samba Shiva Iyyers, popularly known as "Karaikkudi brothers" in Tamilnaadu. The characteristic specialties of Karaikkudi style are:

- Thaala strings are rarely plucked to make the tonal qualities more effective.
- Plucking in the right hand fingers and the skill of the left hand fingers are properly balanced
- Sliding the left hand fingers along the strings to get different notes without discontinuities
- Cross pulling and vibrating the strings in the same steps to render more gamakas
- The vibrations are suddenly stopped by touching the strings with right hand middle fingers (pattu-meetu)
- Play double notes (junty swaras) in thaanams
- Sometimes pluck the three strings together for beautification and attraction.

Popular Vainikas in this style are Karaikkudi brothers, Prof. Subramanyam, Kalpagam Swaminathan, Balaji, and many others.

Bala Chandar's individual style

Sundaram Balachandar, an extraordinary skilled child-prodigy artist in rendering many musical instruments like thabla, mridangam, ganjira, sitar, violin, etc. was performing as accompanying artist at his teen ages (10 to 18 years!). Fascinated by the melodious sound, he suddenly switched over to veena rendering. He learnt veena playing without guidance from any teachers. Due to this, he developed his own very famous Balachandar style by modifying the Karaikkudi style. The specialties of Balachandar's style are:

- Without moving the fingers from the steps, strings are pulled latterly, extensively to raise the notes even up to their octaves, and vibrate frequently to produce enchanting gamakas
- Produce many notes in single plucking
- Pluck the thaala strings very rarely
- Always play veena very slowly in a low, two or two and half shruthis to attract and please the audience.

To implement this technique effectively, Balachandar modified the structure of his veena. He used plastic bridges with a thin stainless steel plate bonded to it as rekhu. This can resist higher deforming forces produced while cross pulling the strings to larger extent. Instead of wooden knobs, he used metal knobs similar ones found in guitar, to change the shruthi quickly. Many artistic carvings are done on the veena for ornamentation. Gayathri Narayan, Madhavan, Jayanthi Kumaresh and many others have studied under him.

Veenai Dhanammal's Style

She became very famous in her time, due to her skill in modifying the Thanjavooru baani. She was applying gamakas abundantly in her own style, and popularized it. She was very expert in linking the different notes through the vibrating notes. Her rendering technique was more related to the slow and medium speeds or tempos (vilambitha and madhyama kaalas). The technique is so complicated that one of the present senior most musicans, Dr. Sripada Pinaka Pani, in appreciation, mentioned, that "it is really a challenge for the artists to master such marvelous techniques!" However, now this style is rarely followed.

Hyderabad-Bobbili –Andhra Baani

As mango trees are available in plenty in Andhra, veenas are prepared using them. The specially decorated types have become famous as Bobbili veenas. Vainikas use vaadaki i.e. instrumental techniques very skillfully in the higher pitches, that is, four or four and half (3 or 4) shruthis, to catch the attention of audience. Very frequent and quick plucking of the main strings with different plucking techniques is used to make the vaadaki style more effective. The thaala strings are also plucked quite frequently. Perhaps this technique was developed due to the influence of the western music and Mysore styles. However, many of the present Vainikas are blending the vaadaki and gaayaki styles (developed by Veene Sheshanna and others, Mysore Baani), which also has great attraction to the present generation.

In this Andhra style, Emani Shankara Shastri has become an international figure. He used to play very skillfully, on two strings simultaneously to produce extraordinary sound qualities and entertain the listeners. His daughter, Emani Kalyani, his disciples Chitti Babu, Pappu Someshwar Rao, and many others like Venkaramana Das, D. Shrinivas, also have become international artists.

Kerala Baani

This is similar to Thanjavooru and Karaikkudi gaayaki (or vocal) rendering styles. To make these baani more effective, the plucking is done at the positions of the Saahithya Aksharas. Chitte thaanams are very frequently rendered. Veena concerts are usually performed in the lower two or two and half shruthis for better tonal effects, which usually pleases the peace loving listeners. Even during thaanam rendering, mridangam accompaniment is sometimes used. Trivendrum Venkatraman, K.S. Narayana Swamy, M.A. Kalyana Krishna Bhagavathar, M.K. Kalyana Krisha Bhagawather, Karamana Parameshwara Bhagavathar, Deshamangalam Subrahmanya Iyyer, S. Rukmini, Shrimathi Gomathi Chidambaram, are some of the well known artists in this baani.

Anantha Padmanabhan's individual style

AnanthaPadmanabhan, perhaps is one of the top-most Vainikas of our country at present. His earlier experiences in sitar rendering in Hindustani style and in orchestra, were utilized for developing his own style. The advantages of the knowledge of the various veena rendering styles, made him to develop his own style. The best aspects of the rhythm controlled gaayaki style and vaadaki styles, skills in plucking and gamaka incorporating techniques, continuity of tonal variations (like that of Hindustani music styles), peculiar combinations of many notes (swara- sangama) as in western music, etc are amalgamated carefully and spontaneously to enrich the concerts. Rendering in low pitches, less plucking, good skills in the movement of left hand fingers,

exhibiting saahithya bhaava and raaga bhaavas with gamakas, playing the higher harmonics in the lower sthaayees, etc, are his specialties. He usually does not tax the audience in the complicated mathematical calculations of renderings. With these techniques, he keeps all aristocratic and present types of audience spell- bound and makes every concert unforgettable!

His son, Anand Kaushik, always accompanying his father in such concerts, was exhibiting excellent skill, and showed all the signs of further bimproving his father's style. But unfortunately he expired at his young age of 36 years which is abig loss to the Veena World.

Shri A Ananthapadmanabhan and Late Anand Kaushik

* * * * *

Chapter - 6

Veena Rendering Specialities-Thaanams and Gamakas

Excellency in veena rendering can be achieved in the first place, by knowing the detailed structure of veena, science of musical sounds, and various complicated rendering techniques, from learned and experienced Gurus, Intensive practice in different varieties of meetus (plucking or strumming), rendering thaanams, fingering skills, inclusion of gamakas etc, is required, regularly, for a long time.

Plucking techniques and varieties

Plucking or "meetu" is the method of striking the strings laterally with the index and middle fingers and suddenly leaving them, when the string vibrates and produces "sound". The plucking makes the string of particular length, under certain tension, to vibrate with definite frequency. This lateral vibrations of the strings produce longitudinal waves in air, which travel with definite velocity (about 333 meters per second) and enter the ears of the listener. The brain interprets it according to its pitch-corresponding to the frequency, loudness- corresponding to the amplitude, and the tonal qualities according to the merger of different harmonics and wave-shapes in the fundamental frequencies. Many plucking techniques are used by the Vainikas skillfully, to produce different sound effects. Normally, index and middle fingers are used for plucking the rendering strings, and small finger is used for plucking the three thaala strings.

Thiruvenkata Kavi had described ten varieties of plucking methods which are; "shrithi, dhara, low, veli (or mael), pattu, edupu, thade, sama, katthari, and laya." Since plucking only produces the sound, he named them as "dasha praanas" (ten lives) of veena. However, even though

many methods of plucking were suggested, only sixteen techniques are now in practice.

1. **Soft (light) meetu:** Very small force is applied for plucking to produce weak sounds of very low energy.
2. **Hard (strong) meetu:** Large force is used while plucking to produce vibrations of larger amplitudes to get louder sounds.
3. **Low meetu:** Plucking is done downwards with index finger.
4. **Veli or mael meetu:** Plucking is done by moving the finger upwards.
5. **Katthari meetu:** Plucking is done, first with index finger and immediately with the middle finger.
6. **Thodu meetu:** Pluck first with index finger and then with the middle finger, separately.
7. **Pattu meetu:** Pluck first with the index finger and stop the sound immediately by touching the string with the middle finger. This is known as 'staccato' in the western music.
8. **Addu meetu:** Pluck first with the index finger, stop the vibration (sound) by touching with the middle finger and immediately pluck again with the middle finger. This technique is used to imbibe the raaga bhaava, saahithya bhava and saahithya aksharas in the gaayaki (vocal-singing) style.
9. **Thaada meetu:** Pluck the string with the middle finger at the third akshara in the thrishra tempo (nade).
10. **Saahithya meetu:** Pluck at the positions of saahithya aksharas.
11. **Abuddaapu meetu:** Pluck the strings where there are no saahithya aksharas. This is for beautification of rendering.
12. **Swara meetu:** Pluck for every notes (swaras).
13. **Koota or ranjana meetu:** Pluck all the rendering strings simultaneously, with three fingers, for beautification.
14. **Gotu meetu:** Pluck all the rendering and thaala strings simultaneously for beautification.
15. **Pakka meetu:** Pluck all the three thaala strings upwards.
16. **Vidi meetu:** Pluck the first three strings (shadja, mandra panchama and mandra shadjas) separately, again, for beautification.

After mastering all these plucking techniques, practice incorporation of various gamakas and the double note (junti- varasas) systems to become a good Vainika.

Thaanam in veena

Thaanam playing is the most attractive, melodious and heart rendering part of all the veena concerts. There are no veena concerts without thaanams. Vainikas show their skills and imaginations (mano-dharmas) in these techniques. Plucking (strumming) of the main strings done with the index and middle fingers one after the other, along with the plucking of thaalam strings with the little fingers in between, rhythmically, to produce sounds anantha-anantha is known as thaanam. The words anantha-anantha represent the Limitless Supreme-Deity.

Thaanams are rendered systematically, usually in the middle tempo, or speed (i.e. madhyama kala) and fast tempo, or speed (dhrutha kala), with separate pluckings for 2, 3, 5, 7, and 9 letters' (aksharas) groups. Vainikas apply low meetu (plucking downwards) on the main strings, and pakka meetu (plucking of the thaala strings) in between the two swaras-pluckings. Some Vainikas render thaanams in slow speed or tempo (vilambitha kala), to get better melody and please the listeners. Since it is quite difficult to pluck the side thaala strings in between rendering the swaras, Vainikas should have good practice and skill. Any confusion will create apa-swaras. For example, if the low and pakka meetus are rendered simultaneously, it will produce Hindusthani style, "Jhaala" of sitar! As thanams are most suitable, they are rendered with the first Ghana raaga panchakas: "Naata, Goula, Aarabhi, Varaali, and Shri" raagas, and also for the second Ghana raaga panchakas: "Saaranga-Naata, Reethi-Goula, Naarayana-Goula, Bhouli and Kedaara raagas".

Thaanams are intelligently rendered quite rhythmically where as raaga- aalapana is rendered freely. One method of rendering thaanams is, initially to play some raaga-related swaras and then thaanams. According to the other method, saahithya (krithi) related thaanam is

first played and then some related swaras are played. While rendering the thaanams, mridangam laya (rhythm) vaadya is sometimes used. This custom is followed in vocal and instrumental concerts in the music festivals conducted at the Navarathri Sangeetha Mantapam of Swaathi Thirunal music college, Thiruvanathapuram. The superb tonal qualities of thaanam rendering in veena with mridangam laya-vaadyas in this manner makes the listeners experience the celestial bliss which cannot be obtained by any other instrumental or even by vocal music! Great musicologist, Dr. Nookala Chinna Sathyanarayana opines that this thaanam rendering technique of veena is followed by the vocalists, since few centuries! and Karnataka classical vocal music improved very much due to veena rendering techinques.

Thaanam- techniques and varieties

Different types of thaanam rendering techniques have been classified for the convenience of identification by the listeners and students:

1. **Eight varieties** according to the walking styles of animals and birds: Manava (man), Ashwa (horse), Gaja (elephant), Markata (monkey), Mayura (peacock), Kukkuta (cock), Mandooka (frog) and Chakra (cyclic) thaanams.
2. **Shuddha** thaanams: This is played with the mela-kartha raagas.
3. **Koota** thaanams: This is used with bhashanga raagas. The swaras have disordered movements that are vakra-sanchaaras.
4. **Sampoorna** thaanams: Rendering with 2,3,4,5 and 6 swaras in different permutation and combinations.

Six varieties thaanams are classified according to their rendering methods:

1. **Chakra** thaanams: Swara bunches (groups) move cyclically.
2. **Vakra** thaanams: Swaras are played in disordered manner.
3. **Mishra** thaanams: All the saptha-swaras are mixed in some orders.

4. **Gambheera** (Majestic) thaanams: The thaanams are played in mandra-sthaayee(low pitch)

5. **Vidyuthaanams:** Thaanams are played in the fast tempo (dhrutha kaala).

6. **Maalika** thaanams: Thaanams are played in different raagas, one after the other, linking them like a chain.

Bharatha has mentioned eighty-four varieties of thaanams! But their details are not available.

Rules followed while rendering the thaanams:

Thaanam rendering scheme (prasthara) should have the following methodical procedures:

1. Thaanam should be played on the jeeva swara(life note) of the particular raagas.

2. During this, the graha swara and the nyaasa swaras, as well as, the raaga characteristics should be remembered throughout.

3. Swara sanchaaras should proceed upwards (aarohana) from the mandra sthaayee(low pitch) to the madhya sthaayee, then on the jeeva swaras and raaga chhaya swaras, and finally ascend to the thaara sthayee.

4. Even in the thaara sthaayee, the swara sanchaaras (note journeys) should be on the jeeva swara, before descending downwards(avarohana) for completing the thaanam rendering.

5. Throughout, maintain the pure raaga-bhaava, rendering technique, skills, as well as, the sustenance of the interest (rakthi, and delight) in the audience.

This system or rules are also followed in rendering the aalapanas!

In Carnatic classical concerts of vocal music, violin, flute, saxophone, naada-swarams, etc, thaanam is optional and is usually rendered as a part of the presentation of the special item, the Raagam- thaanam-pallavis, only. But the Vainikas render many varieties of thaanams in most of the compositions played in the veena-concerts, to present

their skill, raaga bhaava, mano- dharma, etc. Since the thaala strings are also played (plucked) in between, thaanam in veena becomes most attractive and makes the listeners get involved completely. Aristotle had said "that forgetting in the bliss of the melodious music is to realize oneself!"

Gamakas in veena

Indian classical music has many special characteristics and is considered as the best one, in comparison with the other music systems of the world (which have entire written scripts and are followed verbatim). Artists can perform any raaga within its framework, using their own techniques or styles according to their instant emotions (mano-bhaava) and the nature of the audience to expose their talents. In addition, there are many raaga beautification techniques incorporating, vernas, gamakas, swara- prastharas, ornamentation notes, etc, which are sometimes called as swara-alankarana methods. The artist can use these methods according to his mano-dharma, to involve the audience in the same bhaava and rasa states. The gamaka techniques were used even in the Vedic period, while chanting different Vedas. Gamaka is very important in rendering veena concerts for attractive melodious effects. Without gamakas, the notes become plain with the naked swaras!

Gamaka refers to the continuous vibrations of the given sound- notes or swaras, to their higher or lower positions, which is pleasing to listen and make the listeners very happy. Shaarngna (Saranga)Deva, in his "Sangeetha Rathnakara" has stated,

"Swarasya kampo gamakah shrothr chittha sukhaavahah|"

Venkatamukhi, in his "Chathurdandi Prakashike" has explained the gamakas as,

"Swara swaram hi gamakaha shrothr chittha sukhaavahah|
Sweeya sthaana shruthigatha chhaaya hyanyashraya mapi |
Chhaayam gamayathithyesha gamakaha parikeerthithah|"

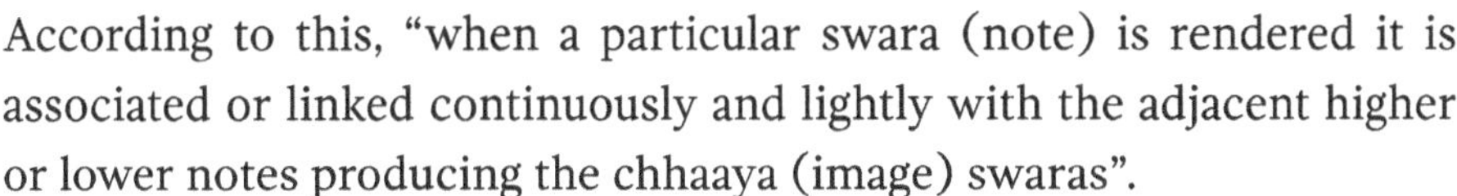

According to this, "when a particular swara (note) is rendered it is associated or linked continuously and lightly with the adjacent higher or lower notes producing the chhaaya (image) swaras".

Paarshwa Deva in his "Samaya Saara" has explained gamakas as:

"Swashruthi sthaana sambhootham chhaayam
shruthyantharaashrayam |
swaroyad gamayedaa geethou gamakoasaa niroopitha|"

The five types of gamakas used earlier, were changed to seven by Someshwara. Shaarngna Deva included eight more and named them as pancha-dasha vidha (fifteen varieties of) gamakas. Musicologist Ahobila mentioned seventeen and later Naarada stated nineteen varieties. This number went on increasing to twenty-two and finally reduced to ten varieties of gamakas, commonly used in practice. This is mentioned by Muthu Swamy Dikshithar in his "Meenakshi mae mudam dehi" verse, in gamaka kriya raaga, while praising the Goddess as "Veena gaana dasha gamaka kriye". However, there is no limit for the number and types of gamakas, Vainikas can use, depending on the situations to exhibit their talents and enriched mano-bhaavas!

Carnatic classical music system commonly uses ten gamakas in practice. (In Hindusthani style also ten gamakas are frequently used). These are: 1. Aarohana, 2. Avarohana, 3. Dhaalu (Soonth), 4. Kampitha-Leena, Aandolitha, Plavitha(Laraja), 5. Ahatha-Rava (Gamaka), 6. Prathyaahatha (Ghaseet), 7. Sphuritha (Jama-jama, Muraki, Geetakadi), 8. Thripuchcha (Masak), 9. Aandolitha (Meend) and 10. Moorchhana. Some of the equivalent names in Hindustani style are given in the brackets.

Saaranga Deva has described 15 varieties, "pancha-dasha vidha gamakas" in his work on music, **"Sangeetha Rathnakara-the ocean of Gems!"** as follows:

"Swarasya kampo gamakah shrothr chittha sukhaavaha|
Thasya bhedaasthu, thirupah, spurithah, kampithasthatha|
Leena, aandolitha, vali, thribhinna, kurula ahathah|
Ullasithah, plavithah, humpitho, mudrithasthatha|
Naamitho, mishrithascha, pancha dashethi prakeerthithah||"

Great exponent of veena, Muthu Swaamy Dikshithar had demonstrated all these "pancha-dasha vidha" gamakas by playing veena and explained their significances and importance of these in the world of classical music. But the gamaka-Thribhinna, is only meant for veena concerts for beautification. This cannot be demonstrated in vocal methods. Naada should be produced in the three tones simultaneously in the Thribhinna gamakas. A Vainika has to press at the positions of vaadi, samvaadi and anuvaadi frets, with the left fingers on the sarane, mandra panchama and mandra shadja strings, and then pluck all the three strings simultaneously with the right hand fingers. To perform this, three vocalists should attempt simultaneously in three tones, which is very difficult. Saraswathi veena is again unique and hence it is the supreme of all musical instruments. Incorporation of gamakas intelligently, is the best method of ornamentation of music concerts. Sundaram Balachander, Veenai Dhanammal, Veene Sheshanna, Thrissur Anantha Padmanabhan and many followers of Thanjavooru bani, give very much importance to these methods.

An old Tamil dictionary, Pingala, has given seventeen names of gamakas especially useful for rendering in veena. These are: Kalithal, Shummai, Kambalai, Irangal, Alungal, Shirambal, Pingal, Thalangal, Karangal, Shilaithal, Thuvaithal, Irathal, Kanaithal, Ishaithal, Imilidal, Emmal, and Ararool. Even though, the details of their structures and methods of rendering are not available, this large number reveals the importance given, as well as, the respect commanded by veena in the society at that time!

* * * * *

Chapter - 7

Veena Naada-Yoga-Salvation

"Naada" is not just the tone. It is the science of sound vibrations even at the micro level in the entire Cosmos. In the philosophical science, Naada is defined by two forms: Aahata Naada and Anaahata Naada

Aahatha Naada

Aahata naada is generated from the external sources in the Universe by way of contact of any two or more physical objects in solid, liquid or gaseous forms. This also can be called as mechanical energy waves which travel to our consciousness through our ears or other senses. The brain interprets these sound vibrations and creates the awareness of tone (naada), pitch (frequency of vibrations), amplitude (loudness), their differences (naada- bheda), identifications, recognitions and also stores these interpretations or experiences in the memory cells. For example, conversations, vocal recital, sounds of string instruments, wind instruments, percussion instruments, etc. produce "aahata naada". All these, certainly carry the emotional vibrations along with the main sound vibrations to the listener. These are inseparables. However, these experiences cannot be explained by merely words. These will have to be realized by the listeners and music lovers. All the sounds we hear or realize in our normal life in this universe are aahata naadas.

Anaahata Naada

In contrary to the aahata naada, anaahata naada is not produced by striking or vibrations of the material objects. This is the unstuck sound and sound of celestial realm. It is found and heard from within the self. Even the breathing has a touch of anaahata sound. This inner sound

can be experienced (or heard) by spiritual practices. This travels from naabhi (navel region) to upwards. Ability to hear this sound is claimed to be the beginning of Kundalini-Yoga. This science is above the physical science and relates to spirituality in the subtle body (Sookshma shareera). Vedas, Upanishads like Thaithireeya, Katha, etc., Yoga Sutras, spiritual literatures, etc. coherently explain the process and relevance of subtle body, brahma-granthi (spiritual knot that clears the illusions when released), naadis (subtle channels) of three types: "sushumna, Ida and pingala", the science of kundalini, six spiritual energy centers-shatchakras, etc.

Energy centres in a Cosmic Body

Realizing and getting immersed in this naada itself is "naadopaasana". The letter "Naa" means praana (life energy) and "Da" means agni (fire element). When the Aatma or praana in our subtle body stimulates the Consciousness, the praana and agni in the Cosmic body (Sookshma shareera), gets united and "anaahata naada flows like a river of energy!" Using this anaahata naada energy, the Yogi (devoted and dedicated practitioner of Yoga) channels the Kundalini energy from mooladhara chakra towards the sahasrara chakra (pineal gland?). The invisible non- material Kundalini energy is believed to be in the form of a coiled serpent facing downwards in the mooladhara chakra located at the pelvis. Awakening it and facing it towards the upward movement is the first step in Kundalini yoga. Then, through persistent saadhana, it is made to flow upwards passing through other energy centers (chakras i.e. swadhistana, manipoora, anaahata, vishuddhi, aajna), and finally unites with the "pranava naada (Om!)" in the sahasraara (pineal gland?). This is equivalent to the Moksha, the state of unlimitted bliss "aananda". All these practices, are possible under the guidance of a learned Yogi or Guru. Only during this practice a saadhaka (practitioner) feels and senses the presence of anaahata naada through the unification of praana and agni "praanaagni". Throughout this process, the balancing of energy channels "ida and pingala with prime channel sushumna" is essential and should be carefully guided by the Guru.

As the Kundalini energy passes through each chakra, the persistent follower experiences some peculiar special divine powers and energies (siddhis). With this, some of the practitioners get attracted to the popularity out of these powers and begin to use them. This deviates them from the path of practice and will soon lose their focus and the special powers. It is said that "Siddhis are obstructions in the spiritual path". The real Saadhaka and Yogi ignore these short term gains (siddhis) and continue to practice this yoga and gains bliss and help the mankind for better and peaceful life.

Limitations of modern science and technologies

Our subtle body has non-material "Brahma-randhra, naadis, shat-chakras", etc. The present material science knowledge, which we call as the modern science, cannot even dream of detecting and studying these subtle and spiritual energies by using modern methods of chemical analysis, advanced technologies using many sophisticated equipments, such as X-rays, Nuclear Magnetic Resonance (NMR), Scattering Electron Microscope (SEM), Atomic Force Microscope (AFM) etc. Though shat- chakras are relatively related to the six glands (it is interesting to note that glands are not connected with nerves and its functioning in response to other activities of the physical body are unknown till date!), it is not yet identifiable through the modern science. All of us are well aware of the fact that, it is not yet possible to explain or measure the physical experiences of our five detecting organs "panchaindrias"; that is, eyes (for observing the colours of objects), tongue (tasting of foods), ears (listening the sounds), skin (feeling of hotness or coldness), and nose (for smelling fragrance), by mere words of any languages in the world with so much advances of science and technologies! One has to experience these with his own organs! Hence, the modern science cannot disregard the spiritual experiences of our ancient yogis, Sadhakas and Thapasvis, just because of its limitations to prove it scientifically using any of the material- made sophisticated equipments! The coherent experiences of Sri Ramakrishna Paramahamsa, Sri Ramana

Maharshi, Sri Aurabindo, and many spiritual sadhakas, even in this era, are documented as strong proof of these invisible energy levels. Hence, some of the material-scientists and the so called rationalists, who disregard these philosophy and spiritual experiences, based on their inexperience, do not surprise the believers of our spiritual traditions.

Vainika and naada-yoga-salvation

In veena recital, when the Vainika plucks the strings without touching any of the frets, sound at mandra sthaayi, at its lowest- energy level is produced from the meruve, that is, its mooladhara. As each fret is pressed, the lengths of the vibrating segments decrease, and the frequencies of the vibrations i.e, the energies of the notes, keep on increasing. When the last (24th) fret is pressed, the distance between the last fret and the bridge (aajna chakra!) becomes the least and the frequency or the energy of vibrations increases to the maximum. At this stage, the sound energy at thaara sthaayi is produced. This highest sound energy travels from the bridge of veena, i.e, aajna chakra, enters the resonator of veena(sahasraara) and gets merged in the pranava (Omkaara). According to the Bhavanopanishath, the following Deity powers are believed to be in each of the chakraas. Chaamundi shakthi in mooladhara, Indraani shakthi in swaadhisthana, Vaaraahi shakthi in manipoora, Vaishnavi shakthI in anaahata, Kaumaari shakthi in Vishuddhi, Maaheshwari shakthi in aajna and Tripura Sundari shakthi in the sahasraara chakras. These are the placements of the saptha-swaras (seven notes in music!). Yogis practice meditating on these divine powers at the corresponding energy centers and attain bliss and many "Siddhis (miraculous accomplishments) or Transcendental powers with respct to their efforts Vainika awakens the Kundalini energy in the mooladhara chakra by combining and channelizing the powers Srf praana and agni (Naa-Da) and unites the Jeevathma (soul) with the Paramaathma (Supreme soul). Vainika's praana shakthi and agni shakthi gets surrounded by the very subtle resonant vibrating sound energies produced by the veena through his fingers and creates celestial vibrations. This elevates the subconscious level of the Vainika to a deeper meditative bliss or moksha (salvation) effortlessly and absolutely. This is spelled by Sri Shankaracharya when he described the veena rendering skill of Goddes Para- Shakthi, with the saptha-swaras, as:

> **"Sa, ri, ga, ma, pa, dha, ni, rathantham veena**
> **Sankrantha kantha hasthantham"**

This is also forcefully declared by the famous sage Yaajnyavalkya in this verse:

"Veena vaadana thathwajnah shruthi jaathi vishaaradah|
Thaala jnaanascha aprayaasena mokshamaarga sagachchathi||"

For attaining salvation (moksha or mukthi) through freedom from all universal or biological bindings, physical actions and consciousness will have to be controlled and channeled through strict and hardest penance (thapas) for a very long time or many years! But a "Vainika having accurate knowledge of shruti (pitch), thaala (rhythm), swara (note or tone) will have an effortless elevation to the path of bliss!" It is frequently observed that even during the early stages of practicing veena recitals, some students with deep concentration on playing, forget themselves momentarily! This state of "untainted with or unaffected by external matters" or "cut-off from the physical world" will keep on increasing as the veena disciple increases the sensitivity towards the shruti, thaala and swara and starts feeling the vibrations of veena within him. At this stage of musical meditation, the "Vainika realizes himself the presence of anaahatha naada in the spiritual centers or the shatchakras!"

The famous Carnatic music Trinities, Naada-Brahma Sri Thyaagaraaja (1769-1847), Muthuswami Deekshithar (1776- 1835) and Shyama Shasthri (1763-1827) were great contemporary Vainikas, vocalists and music composers (vaaggeyakaaras). Their music compositions (krithis) are gems of the music world, with the richness of spirituality,

devotion, emotion, and highest musical qualities. The gist of most complex spiritual and devotional teachings of Vedic literatures and Upanishaths, are greatly woven in their music compositions. These maestros have gifted the music lovers with their divine krithis, music and veena recitals, helping, even the common listener to understand the great values in them and get blessed and blissed. This is one of the famous gems!

"Mokshamu galadaa bhuvilo jeevanmukthulu|
Gaani varalluku sakshaathkara nee sadbhakthi
Sangeetha jnaana viheenaluku
Praana-anala samyogamavalla
Pranava naadamu sapthaswaramulai baraga
Veenaa vaadana loludow Shiva mano-
Vidha merugaru Thyagaraaja vinutha."

(**Note:** According to the Maithravani Upanishad, the "prana" (the inhaled oxygen energy-breath) circulates in the human body, 21,600 times in a day of 24 hours (i.e. 15 times a minute, which agrees with the modern medical sciences!). When our earth completes one rotation, it is our one day. The time taken by the earth to complete 21,600 revolutions is 21,600 days or 60 years, or one "parivruthi." Two parivruthis (known as kalachakram) or 120 years was the life-span (Purusha-ayush) of a normal person at that vedic-period according to Indian astrology. This is considered as two days of sun's life-span. By meditations, the yogis reduce consumption of energy,, i.e. the number of breaths per minute, which is nothing but increasing their life-span. A yogi who recites Gaayathri 100 times, can reduce 21600 breaths to 108 breaths through proper Praanayama, that is, he can increase life-span by 200 times!

It is said that a drop of blood carrying breath energy, requires about 7 minutes for one circulation. When the veena string is plucked, the vibration sound energy moves back and forth between the bridge and the contacted frets, sustains for about 7 minutes. A Vainika yogi

concentrating or meditating on the thaara-sthaayee (at 24th fret), madhya-sthaayee (at 12th fret), or aadhara-shadjams (at meru) sounds within his twelve petelled heart-lotus, can reduces his breaths by 1/10, 1/20 and 1/40th i.e.21,600 to2,160 or 1,080 or 540 times per day, respectively! The yoga of veena rendering in three sthaayees, meditating on the 12 seed syllables(beeja aksharas, ka, kha, ga, gha, nga, cha, chha, ja, jha, nja, tha, thha, in the symbolic twelve petals-heart-lotus (hrudaya-kamala), enhances the life-span of the Vainikas).

A great devotee of Goddess Shri-Vidya, Sri Muthuu Swamy Deekshithar has composed a krithi in "Kamalaa manohari" raaga, named "Kanjadalaayathaakshi...." using beejaksharas (seed syllables) **"ka, ja, tha"** from the twelve letters of symbolic heart lotus with twelve petals and this is believed to be the Saadhaka manthra, for fine arts. Apart from this, with many compositions like "Maamava Meenakshi......", "Meenakshi mae mudam dehi...", etc., Sri Deekshithar has worshipped the Deity for veena, Goddess, Sri Rajamaathangi. Some of the Vainikas believe in securing excellence in veena recital by meditating and chanting "Vipanchya gaayanthi......" the sixty-fifth verse in "Soundarya Lahari" by Sri Adi Shankaraachaarya, everyday thousand times for forty days with some rituals!

Spiritual Energy Centers in Human Body and Veena

Spiritual Energy Centers in the human body are, Mooladhara at Pelvis plexes, Swaadhishtana at Hypogastric plexes, Manipoora at Epigastric plexes, Anahatha at Cardiac plexes, Vishuddha at Carotid plexes, Ajna at Medulla plexes, Sahasrara at Cerebral plexes. Ashtanga Yoga refers to these centers as, Yama, Niyama, Asana, Pranayama, Prathyahara, Dharana, and Dhyana.

Saraswathi Veena corresponds these centers to the placements of the saptha swaras, namely, sa, ri, ga, ma, pa, dha, ni.(at Mooladhara).

1. Mooladhara chakra - Anu mandra note, Ni, is produced behind the Meru of the third string

2. Swaadhishtana chakra - Mandra dhaivatha, dha, is produced in the second string.

3. Manipoora chakra - Madhya Panchama, Pa, is produced at the 7th fret of the first string - Sarane.

4. Anahatha chakra - Thara Madhyama, Ma, is produced at the 17th fret of the first string.

5. Vishuddha chakra - Athi Thara Gandhara Ga, - in between the 24th fret and Ajna chakra in the first string

6. Ajna chakra - Third octave Rishabha, Ri, positioned before the bridge in the first string.

7. Sahasraraa chakra - Shadja below the bridge, in the centre of the Resonator (dome/Kuda).

The frequencies (pitch), or the energies of vibrations, increase accordingly. When the Vainika produces these vibrations by touching these points with his fingers, his Kundalini gets the activating energies by resonance accordingly. The Vainika, as well as the audience, experience the celestial bliss!

* * * * *

Chapter - 8

Varieties of Veenas and String Instruments

Many varieties of string instruments with meaningful beautiful names are frequently mentioned in many Puraanas, history, ancient literatures, poems of the famous poets, etc. However the details of the structures and rendering techniques of few of them are only available. These are some of them:

Thamboora and Thaanpur

This is a basic most important string instrument required for every musician and all Hindustani or Carnatic classical music concerts. This is tuned to the vocalist's natural, most suitable pitch. The continuously vibrating rich tone helps the musician to maintain his tone or pitch (shruthi) and control it throughout the concert. This is a very important support while singing or rendering any instrument. The thamboora used in Carnatic music concerts has a hollow very thin resonator of seasoned jack-wood (or unbreakable fibre), and its dandi is slightly narrow. This is known as Thanjavoor thamboora. The thaanpura has a large gourd shell and the dandi is broader in the Miraj-thaanpur. The lengths are about five or six feet. Three steel and one copper or brass strings tied to the Naaga-pasha-like structure, pass through large plastic beads (for fine tuning), then, grazing over the special curved bridge surface, to the meruve and finally to the rotatable four knobs, which are used for tuning, near the end of dandi. Small hole (naada randhra or Brahma randhra) is drilled below the wooden bridge.

One speciality of these shruthi (drone) instruments is their sustained buzzing sound reverberating with slightly higher notes whose energies gradually decrease! This peculiar effect, commonly called jeeru,

is produced by adjusting a fine cotton, wool, or silk thread in between the strings and the curved surface of the bridge separately. This is the "jeevaala or the soul" of thamboora or thaanpur! When the strings are plucked, they transversely vibrate from the meru to the jeevala, up and down. As the string comes down, it touches softly the nearer part of the bridge surface, reducing the length of vibrating segment, thereby increasing the frequency (pitch). This amplitudes or energies of vibrations (loudness) gradually decrease with time, until the original length of the vibrating segment (i.e. frequency or pitch), is recovered. This causes sudden increase and slow recovery of the pitches of the original notes resulting in the delightful sound (naada!), jeeru -effect. This slightly impure note is closer to the human voice and hence supports the vocalists very well.

The four strings are tuned to mandra panchama, shadja (sarane), shadja (anu-sarane), and mandra-shadja, respectively according to the aadhara shadja. Thamboora is held vertically and the strings are plucked one after the other without touching the other strings. Plucking should be done softly touching the strngs with the skin of finger-tips around the middle of the dandi. The first string (pa) is plucked with the middle finger, a small pause is left, pluck the second and third strings one after the other with the index finger, again leave a small pause, then pluck the fourth string with the index finger. This is rhythmically repeated with a pause continuously. It is a common practice to play two thaanpuras on either sides of the vocalist in the shruthi- based Hindusthani music. The thamboora artists also should have a very extensive practice to render it perfectly in the concerts.

The modern electronic technology is successful in replacing these, to avoid the inconveniences of carrying these large sized structures. Actually larger the size of the thambooras, better is their deep-sound-melody qualities. Also an experienced thamboora artist is required on the stage. Small compact easily portable shruthi boxes are available. These can be tuned very easily, quickly and accurately. Due to this separate thamboora artist is not required. Such many verities of shruthi-boxes are now almost accepted and used during concerts by many artists.

However, the melody, deep sonorous tonal quality, enriching jeeru-effects etc, of the large thambooras cannot be obtained in these innovations. This is like comparing the rich tonal qualities of the large wooden conventional veenas with the electronic versions! Sage Naarada is always associated with thamboora, and the great devotee, Purandara Dasa's famous composition, "Thamboora meetidava, Bhavabhdi daatidava.........Vaikunhtha seridava" is very well-known. The thamboora is also considered as a Divine instrument!

Gottu Vaadyam (Chithra Veena)

This is also known by the names, Hanuman veena, Maha Naataka veena and Chithra veena. In the recent times, this veena is not getting prominence in the Carnatic music. According to one of the puranas (epics), Lord Anjaneya, who was the judge for the veena recital competition between veena experts, Naarada and Thumbura, removed the frets of their veenas and played it by sliding (means gottu in Tamil) a bamboo stick and that too with left hand, producing divine music which was superior than, the veena recitals conducted by Naarada and Thumbura. After this, the veena without frets is called Hanuman veena.

The modern Gottu vaadyam resembles the Saraswathi veena in its structure and is believed to be invented by Sri Sukharaama Rao of Thanjavooru. This has five or six main strings. Usually the first two strings are tuned to madhya-shadjas, third string to mandra-panchama, fourth to mandra-shadja, and the fifth string to anu-mandra-panchamas. There are no frets between the bridge and meru (string holder). It has twelve sympathetic-resonating (melody) strings below the main strings, and has three thaala (rhythm) strings at the side of the dandi (finger board). Thaala strings are tuned to thaara shadja, madhya-panchama and aadhara-shadja from above, respectively. Tuning of the strings is possible through biradai (knobs). Main strings

are plucked by right hand index finger and middle fingers. Thaala strings are plucked by little finger, just like in veena playing. To play raagas by changing notes, thin rods or sticks made up of glass, steel, horns or bamboo, etc, are used by sliding over the strings at different positions to adjust the lengths of the vibrating segments and get the required notes.

This is kept on the floor or mounted on a stand and is played usually at a higher pitches. While playing veena, the strings are pulled across in a controlled method to increase the tension and pitch of the notes. This helps in continuous vibrations of notes and produce ornamentation of notes (gamakas) which causes soothing continuity and divine melody. This technique cannot be used in gottu vaadyam as it has no frets and hence the clarity of the notes, is little lesser in spite of qualitative continuous flow and change of notes. Due to this limitation, more effort and practice is required to play this efficiently. This has led to the decline in its popularity.

The famous maestros of gottu vaadyam in Carnatic music are, Sri Budalooru Krishna Moorthi Shasthri, Mannargudi Savithri Ammaal, Allam Koteshwara Rao, Durgaprasad, Chitra veena Ganesh, etc. Sri Ravi Kiran, grandson of Sri Narayana Iyengar (also a famous gottu vaadyam player), has modified the Chitra veena and is popular all over the world for his Nava Chitra veena recitals

Vichithra Veena

This is similar to gottu vaadyam or Chitra veena and looks like the string instrument veena, but commonly used for accompanying in Hindustani vocal music. It is about six feet long with three feet long flattened teak wood having horizontal arms or cross bars (dandi). This is placed on two large resonating gourds. The ends are decorated with the carving of our national bird, peacock. The string holders are normally made up of Ivory. Four or six main strings are tuned through pegs in the end of the finger board. Below these main strings, thirteen

or fifteen, sympathetic resonating strings are stretched by tuning to the same tensions by the pegs. Apart from these, it has three secondary (chikari) rhythm strings.

Main strings are plucked by index finger and middle fingers. Rest of the strings is played by the little finger to give drone effect. Metal pieces or glass ball is moved (by sliding) on the strings over the finger board by left hand to produce musical notes. Vichithra veena has a range of five octaves. This also has a lesser tonal clarity while sliding over the notes as there are no frets. Comparatively, Vichithra veena is difficult to play and is normally used as accompaniment for Dhrupad style of Hindustani vocal music and is not being used in Carnatic music.

Rudra Veena

According to Shiva-Purana, it was Shiva, who first designed the string veena instrument. He was inspired by the sight of Parwathis' sleeping posture, with her hands covering her breasts! A bamboo column of about six feet in length is fitted to two large hollow gourds of about 14 inches in diameter, with four gut-strings stretched along the length.

This is named as Rudra veena and is popular in Hindustani music. It is one of the largest plucked string musical instruments. Since long time, it was famous as "been or bina" and was used as an accompaniment in Hindusthani music concerts. Now it is made of hollowed wood or bamboo column measuring four and half to five feet in length. This is placed on two large resonators of dried hollow gourds for sound amplification. Twenty four brass frets are fixed on the wooden tube, dandi, with the help of bees' wax. These twenty four frets are to produce twenty four notes. Four main (three steel and one brass) strings and three complimentary (chickaree) strings are stretched along. Pegs are provided to tune the strings. To produce base or deep sound, bigger gourds and thicker strings (0.45 mm or 0.47 mm or 26 or 25 gauges) are used.

Pandit Lalmani Mishra modified this traditional Rudra veena to play Bharatha's shadja graama and twenty two shrutis.

Mohan Veena

The lone Indian winner of the prestigious Grammy award for music, Pandith Vishwa Mohan Bhat, was inspired by the popular string instruments, veena, sitar, and sarod, for fabrication of this hybrid string instrument which he named after him. This looks like a guitar as its wooden resonator is of similar shape of guitar. It has three main strings, five drone strings and twelve resonating strings. These are tuned by separate pegs. Some artists play this instrument by keeping this on their laps and some hold it vertically. Mr. Salil Bhatt, further modified his father's (Vishwa Mohan Bhatt's) Mohan veena and popularized his "Satvik veena.

Veenas cited in the ancient Indian scriptures

Hundreds of names of string instruments called as veenas, are available in the ancient Indian scriptures and history. However, the details of their designs and techniques of playing are not known. The literature, "Sangeetha Rathnakara" by Saranga (Sharngna) Deva, describes some of the veenas. By analyzing these details, the stage by stage development of designs and techniques of veena can be figured out. This analysis will throw light on the evolvement of complete and perfect "Saraswathi" veena which is most popular at present. The following are some of the veenas during this evolvement process, gathered from various sources.

Eka-thanthri Veena

It is made of red Sandalwood (Raktha Chandana) measuring 35-36 inches in length. It has tubular shape and is hollow. One side is placed on wooden resonator and the other side has decorative Yali face (head). The tubular portion narrows down towards the head.

Alaapini Veena

This is also made of Red Sandalwood and has length of about thirty six inches. The tube has very small circumference of about two and half inches. Instead of the gourd, it has coconut shell. In place of metal strings, strengthened silk thread is used to produce good tone for aalaapanas in music concerts. That is the reason for its name "Aalaapini". This veena, carved in the idols of instrumentalists in the temples of Badami, has two gourds and single string. The shila-balikas (stone sculptures) in the Mahalaxmi temple of Doddagaddavalli, has one wooden and another gourd resonators

Kinnari Veena

According to the Hindu mythology, Kinnari means a celestial usician with upper body of female human and lower body of a horse. Kinnara is male gender. In the great epics, Ramayana and Mahabhaaratha, there are descriptions of Kinnaras, Kinnaris, Yakshas and Gandharvas, residing in the Himalayan range in the northern India, who were good at fine arts, dance, music, veena etc. Even the cultures of Thailand, Cambodia, Philippines, Burma, etc. which have great influence of Indian Culture, have traditional heritage linkages to dance and drama of Kinnaras, Kinnaris, their sculptures and fables about them, etc. Veena played by Kinnaris is called Kinnari veena. The wooden hollow tube is of about thirty-five to fifty three inches length, five inches wide, two and half inches height. It is placed on three wooden resonators. The bridge has rekhu, (pathrika) made of brass (now steel is used) and fourteen frets made up of copper are placed systematically on the tube with the help of bees' wax. This produces notes in two octaves. Saranga Deva has described the technique of playing this. The main strings are plucked by the right fingers and left fingers are used to press the positions of frets to get right notes.

This traditional, ancient Kinnari veena has a history of thousands of years. The description of Kinnari veena, design and its techniques of playing resemble the modern Saraswati veena. There are different types

of Kinnari veenas based on their sizes: Brihati Kinnari (fifty three inches long), Madhyama Kinnari (forty three inches long) and Laghu Kinnari (thirty five inches long). The width and heights are proportional to their lengths. The naaga-paasha, bridge, rekhu, are all similar to those of Saraswathi veena. According to Haripaala Deva, fourteen, sixteen and eighteen fretted Kinnari veenas resemble the stringed instrument, sitar!

Pinaaki Veena

The famous bow of Lord Shiva is called Pinaaka (Shiva is named Pinaaka Pani). This Pinaki veena is bow shaped and the tube has length of about one meter. It measures approximately seven cms, width in the centre and four cms, thick at the ends. This is held vertically and played with a bow instead of plucking. The present string instrument, "Dilruba" might have been evolved from the Pinaaki veena. The description and types of strings are not available.

Some presently used string instruments

1. Sitar

During the Vedic period and even earlier, in the ancient India, all the string instruments were known as veenas. There were different types of veenas, like Eka thanthri, Dwithanthri, Thritanthri,-----etc, depending on the number of strings. Historically, it is believed that sitar is descended from the Persian instrument "Seh Tar" meaning three strings. During the Moghals' rule in India, Amir Khusroo brought this 'Seh Tar' from Persia and popularized it. However, there is a vast difference between the Seh-Thar of Moghals' period and the current Indian sitar. Though sitar is used in Hindustani music, it resembles the twenty-four fretted and seven stringed Saraswathi veena in terms of structure, playing techniques, etc. According to Manchaala Jagannatha Rao, sitar is one of the forms of "Eka raaga swara mela Saraswathi veena". Haripala Deva opines that sitar is a form of Kinnari veena.

Main comparisons between Veena and Sitar

1. Both veena and sitar look alike.
2. Veena has wooden resonator, while, sitar has gourd resonator.
3. Both have nearly same lengths.
4. At the other end of fret-boards they have decorative wooden resonator or Thumba of gourd.
5. Pegs are provided similarly, to tune the strings.
6. Both have four main strings, three thaala strings.
7. There are about thirteen or fourteen secondary strings (sympathetic strings) stretched under the main strings which are controlled by the pegs in the sides of the fret-boards.
8. Similar to naaga-paasha in veena, sitar has langot at one end to fix, or tie the strings.
9. Veena has twenty four straight brass frets fixed to the wax rails on the fret-board at definite positions. Sitar has fifteen or eighteen curved brass frets tied to the metal rails with the hardened silk or nylon threads in shiftable positions. These are used to change the length of the vibrating segments of the strings, to get required notes in both.
10. Just like Eka raaga swara mela veena, sitar is also an Eka raaga swara mela string instrument. Positions of the frets are to be shifted in both the cases to get the required notes according to the particular rendering raagas. Hence, every time the raaga is changed, the fret positions are required to be changed; even the sympathetically-resonating strings also should be tuned accordingly.
11. There are many similarities in the techniques of plucking, playing, tension controlling, incorporation of gamakas etc.

The curvature of the frets in sitar is one of the main reasons for the difference in sound quality in comparison to the straight frets of veena. The curved frets of sitar facilitates the easier movements of strings sideways while being plucked, pressed, and vibrated laterally. This results in the greater changes in the lengths of the vibrating segments

of the strings and thus producing greater amount of higher harmonics components in the same frets. This richness of higher pitch- tonal sound quality of sitar is also due to the resonance created by the many sympathetic strings, merging with the notes and its harmonics produced by the main strings. This has added to the popularity of sitar. It may not be possible to produce such attractive note variations of sitar, in veena. But, it is a fact, that it is not possible to get the deep sonorous quality, divine melody, majestic tonal richness and bliss of veena-naada from any other musical instruments.

2. Soor-Shringar

This is a hybrid structure of Rabab, Mahathi veena and Kachchapi veenas! This has gourd resonator (like mahathi veena), metal sheet on the finger board (like rabab) and flat finger board(like Kachchapi veena). This has four main strings, two thaala strings, tuning knobs and steel plectrum (mizraab). It is used and played like sarod. As the rendering technique is complicated, there are very few Soor Shringar artists at present.

3. Soor Bahar (Lower or Mandra Sitar)

This has similar structure and appearance as sitar, but of still larger size, prepared around 200 years ago, by a been- player, Uma Rau Khan. The finger board is semi-circular with flat bottom. The strings are thicker to produce lower pitch or mandra sthaayee notes and better deeper melody. Number of strings, tuning and playing methods are all similar to sitar rendering

4. Rabaab

This is prepared by hollowed wood. The resonator is covered with goat's skin membrane and the other part near the finger- board has wooden lid. There are four or six strings, (all of guts or two of brass) and has no frets. It is played by using metal plectrum or by bowing methods.(The rebeck instrument in Persia and Arabia is similar to Rabab). It is said that great musician Thaansen was also playing rabaab.

5. Sarod

This might have been structured by slight modifications in the rabab. Asadulla Khan was using this about 100 years back in Bengal. One end of this is semi-spherical hollow wooden part of about 25 cms, width which gradually decreases to about 7or 8 cms, in a length of about 100cms. The upper part is covered with stretched leather and carries a bridge. Above this and finger-board, there are six (including chikaari) strings used for playing, and 11 or 12 resonating tharab strings whose tensions can be adjusted. Using metal plectrum, strings are plucked in right hand and the notes are obtained by pressing them on the finger-board according to the raagas. Mandra-sthaayee notes are reverberating, maddhya and thaara-sthaayee notes have peculiar intensities! Alaap, Jzod, Jhaalas can be played melodiousy. Even though sarod is played as solo instrument, it is more suitable to enrich the fusion music. There are many internationally well-known sarod players.

6. Saarangi

This is made up of a solid single piece of wood of about 60 to 65cms in length covered with a stretched leather. There is a bridge carrying four rendering strings (three of guts and one brass). In the modern saarangi, there are about 30 to 40 resonating (tharab) strings, stretched at desired tensions, below the main strings. Saarangi is played with bow, holding vertically supporting on the left shoulder like violin. This gives melodious note variations (gamakas) and is used for solo or as good accompaniment for Hindusthani music.

7. Dilruba

This is a combination of Sitar and Saarangi structurally. The finger-board, brass frets and their adjustments (separate for different raagas: Eka- raaga-swara mela veena) and left hand rendering are like that of sitar. The resonator is wodden hollow structure shaped like that of saarangi and has a bridge. The 18 or 19 frets are tied with guts. The main and tharab strings are tuned differently for various raagas. This is

used for solo but more frequently as accompaniment for Hindusthani music as well as in fusion-music. Isa-raja and Mandra-bahar are similar to Dilruba and belong to the same class of bowing instruments. These are rarely used for obtaining the lower pitch-mandra sthayees.

8. Santhoor

This was known as shatha-thanthri veena in Sanskrit and its versions in Greek is Santouri, and in Chinese is Yangain.

It is also similar to the swara mandala string instruments. This has trapezoidal (or rectangular) shaped hollow sound box of mulberry, walnut or maple wood covered by its or plywood thin sheet. There are 75 to 100 strings of steel and copper(or brass) stretched between row of nails at one side and another row of 26 to 29 rose-wood bridges (with ivory plates) on the other side. These strings have different lengths. These are grouped in three or four in numbers for different notes, passed through different bridges and tuned by tuning pegs behind the bridges. Two, very light sticks(mallets or mezrab) with oval or serpant's hood shaped ends, are held between the index and middle fingers to strike the various strings tuned to required notes. Tones of different types are produced when the strings are struck near or away from the bridges. The steel strings are tuned to higher pitches. Striking by the left hand is accompanied by the striker of right hand or sometimes with the fingers. (Sound is produced in Swara-mandala by plucking). The player sits in ardha-padmasana, places santoor on his lap with its long side towards him. This is rendered in Hindustani style. Pandith Shiva Kumar Sharma is a famous santoor player.

9. Guitar

Guitar is multi- stringed instrument (Cithara in Latin), having quite a long history, since 13th or 14th centuries in the European countries. This appears like a huge violin with a large very thin hollow sound box, a bridge and a long finger-fret board.. There are usually six strings (sometimes 4-18), nineteen metal-frets (sometimes 21-24) on the fret-board and tuning pegs at the other end of it. These frets are fitted according to mathematical formulations (almost similar to fret- fixing in veena). Large sound-holes are made in the sound box for amplification. Nowadays electrical pick-ups are common. The plucking or strumming is done with plectrums or right hand fingers and rendering (finger-pricking) is done with the left-hand fingers. Guitar is a very popular common accompanying instrument in Hindusthani style light music and fusion music concerts. Recently some are introducing guitar in Carnatic classical music, light music and fusion music concerts

10. Mandolin

Mandolino in Italian is also a stringed instrument used in the western countries since a long time. This also has a hollow thin resonator tear-drop shaped sound box with sound-f-holes, bridge, finger-fret-board, tuning pegs etc. There are mainly three varieties; round bowl-back resonator (prepared from a thin hollow wood), curved top and flat back (made by joining thin sheets of wood). Four-paired i.e. eight strings pass over the 18 to 20 frets fitted on the fret-finger-board which are commonly tuned by pegs to E.A.D.G. like violin strings (For example; E5=660 or 659.25, A4=440, D4=293.66, and G3=196 Hz.). Tuning can be done in many varities as required. Playing is done like guitar.

In India, mandolin always is associated with Master U. Shrinivas who introduced it to Carnatic classical music for the first time. He was an exceptional child prodigy. At the age of five years, he modified a bowl shaped mandolin by using five, single-stranded strings and twenty-four frets and played it like a veena! Within seven years, he was able conduct superb masterly major concerts! His debuts very soon got publicized and this was easily accepted for Carnatic classical music within ten years! But the present very popular violin, introduced by Varahappa Iyer, Balu Dikshithar and Vadivelu, 200 years back to Carnatic classical music took almost one century for acceptance! Shrinivas soon became very popular exhibited his skill in many western countries several times and got the appreciation from those audience who considered him next

to the great Pandith Ravi Shankar. "Padma Shri" was awarded to him in1998. He brought out many mandolin recital albums. Unfortunately he passed away in Sept.2014 after undergoing liver transplantation.

11. Violin (Viola)

This version of fretless string instrument was known as Dhanur-veena and also as Ravana Hastha veena in India since long time. It was a very popular stringed bowing instrument in the western countries since long time. This entered India perhaps, along with the British East India Company and became popular very soon. A minister, Varaha Appayya procured this for the King of Thanjavoor. It is said that Muthu Swamy Dikshithar brought violin from north India. Rendering was mastered in the Carnatic classical style and very much publicity was given by his brother Balu Swamy Dikshithar, and also by Vadivelu. But it took a long time of about a century for accepting as Solo and aaccompaniment to Carnatic vocal classical concerts! Swathi Thirunal Maharaja gifted a special ivory violin to violinst Vadivelu. As violin is very popular and known to all musicians and music- lovers, only a brief description is given.

These are prepared by very skilled artisans as cottage industry in many countries, like, Italy, Germany, France etc and now prepared in Calcutta, Jayapur, Trivandrum and in few other places in India. Stradivarius, Guameri, Ameli, Montagnano, etc, are the standard names. The waist shaped, very thin sound box (similar to guitar) is prepared by joining the front and back parts (of maple or pine trees), through a small sound post (of maple wood) in between, for communicating the sound from the strings via the bridge. Four strings of plain steel and twisted aluminium, or electro-metal are used. These four strings (E.A.D.G.), are usually tuned to madhya-panchama, madhya-shadja, mandra- panchama, and mandra-shadjas, respectively. Normally, there are four strings, but nowadays five or six strings are also used. Famous, Mysore Peteel Choudayya was expert in playing in seven stringed violins! Violins of different sizes are prepared for the conveniences of the users like small children. The full- size is of 14 inches (35.6 cms), three fourth size is of 13 inches (33.5 cms), half-size is of 12 inches (31.0 cms) etc body-lengths. Still smaller $\frac{1}{4}, \frac{1}{8}, \frac{1}{10}, \frac{1}{16}, \frac{1}{64}$ th are also available. The bows used have about 75 cms length, 60 gms, weight, and the strings are of grey or white coloured male horses'tail-hairs and nowadays of synthetic fibers.

Viola is only a larger sized violin, of body lengths 37 to 43 cms. The four strings are sometimes tuned as C.A.D.G. Viola produces little deeper (bass) sound as it has larger dimensions. This has not gained much popularity.

Golden age for violin

This is a golden-age for violin! It is played as solo, and is an inevitable essential accompaniment in almost all varieties of classical vocal, light, fusion music programs, Bharatha Natyams etc. There are thousands of professional expert violinists flourishing very well in India and many foreign countries! Hundreds of them have become internationally recognized violinists. Earlier, before the invasion of violin to the Indian classical music world, about hundred years back, veena was dominating as it was considered as the most suitable accompaniment for Carnatic classical vocal music due to its rich tonal quality being closest to the human voice. Similarly veena was used as the essential accompaniment to all the classical Indian dances like Bharatha Natyams, Mohini Attam, Koochuppudi etc, as its melodious tones can assist the artists to express their sahithya- bhava emotions more effectively! However due to many reasons already explained, veena has lost its dominence to the violin, even though violin is not actually so much suitable due to lower melody.

Melody and sound delight of string and other musical instruments

When the lengths of the strings are reduced below, about 35 inches (85 cms.), the melody and naada-soukhya (sound- delight) of the

stringed instruments decreases. This is because, the fundamental frequencies of the vibrating strings increase when the lengths of strings are reduced. Along with this, the energies and number of overtones increase. Due to this, the distortion of the sine wave forms also increases resulting in the reduction of deep base tones. Thus the string instruments which are smaller in size, like violin, sarod, mandolin, guitar, etc, produce tones that are less deep less bass and have higher pitch qualities due to the presence of higher energy components of the harmonics, matching with the female voices. These are sometimes known as female instruments. For this reason, the lengths of the string instruments like thamboora (thaanpura), veena, sitar, etc, are maintained longer and size of their resonators bigger, in spite of the problems of transportation.

Likewise, longer the bansuri (long flute for the Hindustani music type), clarinet, saxophone, etc. have deep majestic (Gambheera!), bass sound qualities, while, the short, shehnai has more higher-pitch components and produces shrill notes! Avanaddha vaadyaas, (percussion instruments) also have these limitations. The lengths of the vibrating air columns and volumes of air in the resonating parts, produce the tonal quality in proportion to their increase of sizes. Lengthy strings and bigger resonator of veena, give the higher quality of sound melody (musical delight) and tones (naadas). This makes the involvement of the Vainikas and the listeners (shrothru) with dedication, merging the soul (Atma) with the Super Power (Parama-Atma) through merging of the vibrations of **Aahatha and Anaahatha Naadas i.e. Naada-Yoga!**

* * * * *

Chapter - 9

Famous Vainikas

Vainika Shikhamani, late, Mysore Veene Sheshanna

Veene and Sheshanna are inseparables. Even the world famous Mysore is a part of this great unity. This union has a great influence and impact on the popularity and tradition of Carnatic classical music in India. During the rule of the Kings of Mysore in the 19th century, there were many great musicians, music exponents, violinists and vainikas in Mysore. For this reason, well-known poet, B.M. Shri. had proclaimed that "Veeneya bedagadu Mysooru" in his poem, meaning Mysore is the glory of veena, might be keeping Vainika Shikhamani Veene Sheshanna in his mind. Most revered awards of those times, like "Shikhamani, Aasthana Vidwaan, Bhakshi", etc, were showered upon Veene Sheshanna. He was well known to and well respected by not only the veena artists but also all musicians since then throughout India. "If veena is played, it should be played like Veene Sheshanna" is the most common wish of all. He was the best role model musician, artist, and wizard of veena, crest jewel of music, eminent composer, exponent Naadopaasaka, exemplary Karma yogi and a treasure of classical music! He dedicated his life for veena. He explored, developed and practiced all the possibilities of playing techniques of veena and contributed to the classical music, the famous style "Mysore Baani'. He was a prodigy, still a hard practitioner, expert musician, still experimental by nature, well recognized still simple living, a vainika but also expert player of various string instruments and jalataranga, profound scholar, sincere and dedicated, humble, filled with humility and believed that music is superior to artists! His life achievements and rigorous practice, are exemplary and inspiration to all musicians and music students.

Genealogy of Veene Sheshanna

The prominent personality in the genealogy of Veene Sheshanna was Pachimiriam Aadi Appaiah, who composed a varnam "Viriboni ninne kori", in Bhairavi raaga and atta thaala, which is supposed to be a challenge to musicians. The other stalwarts like Kuppaiah, Somanna, and Veene Sambaiah are well known in this lineage. During those days, Veene Sambaiah was the most popular musician and people believed that Lord Samba (Shiva) would be pleased only with the veena playing by Sambaiah. His son was the great composer, Veene Kuppaiah. Veene Venkatasubbaiah was the son of Veene Kuppaiah. His son, Veene Dodda Sheshanna was the veena teacher of Veene Sheshanna and father of another veena expert, Vainika Praveena, Bhakshi Subbanna. Veene Kuppaiah's daughter's son, Veena Bhakshi Chikkaramappa was the father of Veene Sheshanna. Veene Sheshanna adopted Ramanna, whose son is the well- known Swaramoorthi, V.N. Rao and grandson is Mysore V. Subrahmanyam. Thus the genealogy of Veene Sheshanna itself is full of veene virtuosos. Many famous music personalities, Aasthan Vidwans of Mysore and Tanjavoor Kingdoms, Vainikas, Violinists were disciples of Veene Sheshanna. Mysore Sadashiva Rao, Karigiri Rayappa(Rao), Mysore Vasudeva Aachar, Veene Sambaiah, Venkata Subbaiah, Chikka Ramappa, Dodda Sheshanna, Dodda Subba Rao, Chikka Subba Rao, Sheshanna, Venkatagiriappa, Lakshminarayanappa, Padmanabhaiah, Veene Subbanna, Chandrashekaraiah, Bidaram Krishnappa, Devendrappa, T. Chowdaiah, are a few jewels of classical music during the regime of Mysore Kingdom. Thus everyone recalls musicians, Vainikas, Violinists and Veene Sheshanna along with Mysore!

Childhood and education of Veene Sheshanna

Veene Sheshanna was born in 1852 to Bhakshi Chikka Ramappa, an Aasthana Vidwan of Mysore Maharaja Mummadi Krishnaraja Wodeyar's time. This great father was the first tutor of Sheshanna by initiating him to music and laid strong foundation to shruti, swara and laya. At the tender age of ten years, child- prodigy Sheshanna presented a complex Pallavi before the King and Aasthan Vidwans in response to the challenge by a musician of Thanjavoor and won accolades from everyone and also was presented with a studded necklace from the King himself. At that age itself, Sheshanna had exhibited his virtues, expertise and ambition to become a complete musician. He lost his father and mother at the age of 11 years and was taken care of by his elder sister, Venkamma. She had a great affection towards Sheshanna and was instrumental in bringing up the best of Sheshanna. Sheshanna continued his vocal music learning under the guidance of great composer and Aasthan Vidwan, Mysore Sadashiva Rao. Later Sheshanna started learning veena playing at the age of eighteen years, under Dodda Sheshanna, Aasthan Vidwan of Mysore, who was the disciple of Sheshanna's father. Dodda Sheshanna's son, Veene Subbanna was also a great Vainika and they became good friends. Later, the famous vocalists, Bidaram Krishnappa, Mysore Vasudeva Aachar and many others became close friends of Veene Sheshanna.

Dodda Sheshanna was a devoted strict teacher. Unless the lessons taught are rendered perfectly, he wouldn't continue with the next lessons. Once, he taught begade raaga to Sheshanna. When, in spite of 4-5 days of practice, Sheshanna couldnot get his Guru pleased with the mastery over that raaga, the teacher himself played it in all the six speed scales. Sheshanna was taken aback by a great surprise and shed tears of immense joy. Sheshanna strongly believed in his Guru's mandate that "music is the asset of extensive and persistent practitioner. Every raaga and thaala should be practiced over hundred times and should be mastered!"

Venkamma: Mentor of Sheshanna

Sheshanna's elder sister Venkamma was instrumental in the making of veena maestro in Sheshanna. She had an in-depth knowledge of music and had a built- in desire to make Sheshanna a world famous

Vainika. She steered his music practice, guided, monitored and mentored him throughout his journey of music. When Sheshanna was getting tutored under Dodda Sheshanna and Sadashiva Rao, she personally supervised his practice and insisted strict conditions for practice sessions, ranging from morning 3 a.m. till 6 a.m. Then he was sent for lessons from Gurus till 12 noon and again, the practice sessions continues till evening 6 p.m., was the daily routine. Daily six varnas, twenty five compositions (krithis), thaanams in Ghana raagas, two pallavis were part of the compulsory practice sessions, without completing which, Sheshanna was not allowed to sleep and even take food! This may be scary news for the modern music students but is the real proof of the old saying "success follows hard work". Venkamma used to be present during his practice sessions and every concert. She guided him with strict criticisms and defects in shruti, laya and raaga presentations, thus making him a flawless musician. In spite of the praise from all the audience, Sheshanna wouldn't have got satisfied until he gets a nod from sister Venkamma. This kind of guidance, monitoring and mentoring by Venkamma, was a blessing to Sheshanna, to become a great personality in music and to develop his own style in veena playing.

Family of Sheshanna

Kashibai, the first wife of Sheshanna, died untimely and two children from her also died early. Since Sheshanna had no children from the second wife, Subbamma also, he adopted Ramanna, brother of Subbamma. Due to these unfortunate incidents, Sheshanna lost his interest in the worldly attachments and became introvert. He devoted himself to music and veena teachings to selected disciples. He spent his entire time, in religious rituals, philosophical thinking and playing veena for the interested audience, whenever he was requested.

Purusha Saraswathi Sheshanna

Sheshanna, in addition of being a veena exponent, was also an expert in vocal recital and in many musical instruments. He used to conduct

"Krishnotsava" at his residence for about 10 days continuously to fulfill the lacunae he felt with the "Raamotsava" in Mysore. People and musicians thronged the place and were involved in all the programmes without any breaks. They used to enjoy every minute of this music fest which included concerts of vocal, veena, flute, violin, sitar, piano, swarabath, jalatarang, classical dances, etc. Sheshanna himself used to play various instruments on these days, if there were less number of musicians for the concerts. He used to play veena in different styles like, rigid rhythmic (laya) style of Carnatic music, enchanting free style of Hindusthani renderings, peculiar note combinations (swara - sangamas) of the Western fusion music, etc. on these occasions. Even if he had played the same raaga at different times, it would sound different and special, according to his mano-dharma (emotional state of mind), style of playing, involvement of audience, with varieties in swara sancharas, tonal displays, etc.

Once, Ustad Allabhaksh played Jalatarang in the court (durbar) of Mysore King and challenged the Aasthana Vidwans. Sheshanna bought clay bowls and prepared Jalataranga by filling them with water, practiced for 3 days and played varnas, krithis, thillaanas, in the King's durbar relentlessly. Witnessing this astonishing performance by Veene Sheshanna, Ustad Allabhaksha praised him and made a statement that he need not come to Mysore anymore!

King of Ramanathapura, Bhaskar Sethupathi, had arranged veena concerts by Sheshanna throughout all the nine days of Navarathri festival. Sheshanna had presented concerts in various parts of our country, like, Baroda, Gadval, Gwalior, Bhopal, Pudukkottai, etc. and got felicitated all over. He would have been world famous, if he had given performances abroad. However, he did not travel abroad, as crossing the sea was prohibited by the philosophy in which he had belief. Most of the music maestros of that time, like, Maha Vaidyanath Iyer, Sharabha Shastry, Pudukkottai Dakshina Moorthy, Thirokkodikaval Krishna Iyyer, Veenai Dhanammal, etc, have praised Sheshanna's skills and honoured him.

Once, Mysore Maharaja arranged to take Sheshanna in the royal palanquin with royal procession through the streets of Mysore to honour him. Sheshanna, a sincere devotee of Veena, placed the veena in the palanquin and walked alongside the procession and showed to world that veena is superior to the artist. This reflected his humble personality and devotion towards Divine Veena. He used to play veena without reference to time and number of people, whenever requested, with a feeling that it is his pleasure to play veena!

Emotional attachment and involvement in veena recital

Sheshanna used to forget himself often during the veena recital because of deep involvement, high level of devotional and emotional attachments, in this raaga-anusandhaana (oneness with the raaga) and naada yoga. Sometimes, he used to stop playing, at the peak of the emotions declaring "I have played only to the extent of my limitations. Is it possible to play to the fullest extent of the capacity of veena? I could not understand the depth of veena till now. How much penance, (thapas) is required to get the blessing of veena to be an expert? With these humble statements he used to embrace veena emotionally and reflected his attachment to the Divine Veena.

Once, during his concert in the famous Parthasarathi temple at Triplicane, Madras (Chennai), thousands of people were grossly involved in the musical melody. At that time, a serpent (Shesha in Hindu philosophy) appeared from nowhere and was seemingly absorbed in the veena-naada vibrations for about forty five minutes by swinging its expanded hood rhythmically and vanished likewise! Even though the audiences were scared, Sheshanna never noticed this and was involved in veena playing only. After being told about this, his reaction was that his home–deity "Shesha" had blessed him in the form of, serpent God, Maha Shesha.

During those days (beginning of twentieth century), the modern sound technology like microphones, amplifiers and loud speaker systems were not available. It is unbelievable, even though true, that the melody and divine tunes of veena, are made to reach thousands of people in open auditoriums, without the help of sound amplifying systems and make them engrossed with the veena naada. This, itself reflects the power of music and veena.

Sheshanna, played veena with complete dedication, devotion and spread the divinity of veena to lakhs of people until his death bed. Even when he was on the death bed, he used to look at his veena kept beside him and shedding tears in praise of it. He passed away on 25th July 1926 leaving his name immortal in the saga of Carnatic music.

Great composer-Sheshanna

Sheshanna had composed many scholarly Swarajathis, Varnas, Kritis, Keerthanas, Thillanas, Jaavalis, etc. in different raagas and thaalas. He used the pen–names, "Shesha and Sheshadaasa" in his compositions. Some of his compositions are not popular due to the intricacy and complexity to render them. Some are very much popular amongst dedicated music lovers. Some scholarly musicians are attracted by some of his thillanas. Amongst these thillanas, the one in raaga "janjooti" has become very famous. His thillana compositions are very special and some are especially composed for Bharatha Naatyam which is of rare kind and very enthralling.

Honours and felicitations

During the lifetime of Sheshanna, there were no advanced communications, television media, print media, publicity activities etc, and even the travelling and transportation was a challenge. Also the numbers of music organisations which recognized and felicitated music wizards were limited. No Government sponsored or politically initiated or organized by vested interest organizers were present during those period. However, many Kings and music lovers got mesmerized by Sheshanna's performances and showered upon him many silk shawls, diamond rings, gold bracelets, gold chains felicitating his scholarly knowledge and achievements. In 1902,

during the coronation of Mysore Maharaja, King accorded him the title "Vainika Shikhamani" meaning crest jewel of all vainikas, which was the highest honour of those days. Thus, the life and achievements of Veene Sheshanna is inspirational and role model to all music lovers.

Late Sundaram Bala Chander

Born in 1927 to late Sri Sundaram Iyer and late Shrimathi Parvathi in Mylapore, Chennai, Sundaram Bala Chander was a child prodigy in classical music. He was a khanjira (percussion instrument) player at the tender age of six years and was giving performances as an accompaniment! At the age of fifteen years, he became an expert musician in playing mridangam, thabla, bulbul tharang, dilruba, shehnai, harmonium, etc, and played all these instruments as accompaniments to the artists of Madras All India Radio station, till the age of eighteen years. He also learnt sitar and Hindustani music as well!

At the age of eighteen years, he got attracted to divine veena and started learning veena on his own, without the help of any Guru. He practiced rigorously and mastered the playing technique of veena and developed his own style within two years and started veena concerts as a full-fledged artist! Since, he had no influence of any particular baanis or Gurus, he could come out with his own style, full of enriching gamakas and tonal variations. He used to play veena and sitar also in Hindustan style and western styles and became popular for his new "Bala Chander Style", named after him.

He performed many concerts of classical music, fusion music, and symphony with western musical instruments in many countries of the world and made veena popular in those countries. He had played and recorded all the 72 melakartha raagas (janaka raagas) of Venkatamukhi. These recordings became popular and standard all over the world and gave much publicity to the Divine Veena and its power of music. Multi talented Bala Chander has composed and directed music for many Tamil and Thelugu films. In 1982, he was honored with "Padma

Bhushana" award by the Government of India. He passed away in 1990 when he visited Bhilai to give a concert.

Late Emani Shankara Shastri

Emani Shankara Shastri was born in 1922, in Andhra Pradesh, to Vainika Bhushana, Veena Acharya, Emani Achyuta Shastri. Famous Vainika Sangameshwara Shastry and Veena Venkatarama Dasa are his contemporary artist Shankara Shastri was tutored by his father under the strict practice and guidance. He gained extra-ordinary skill in special playing technique of veena and became popular all over the world. He became well known in north India, where Hindustani music is popular, by giving joint performances (Jugalbandhis) with various string instrument players of Hindustani styles. He is known for his contribution in developing and popularizing the famous "Andhra (Hyderabad) baani" which is the instrumental (vaadaki) style. He was accorded with the honorary Doctorate by the University of Andhra Pradesh.

He has directed and composed music for many films of Thamil and Thelugu in Gemini Pictures of Madras (Chennai). He has given numerous performances in All India Radio. He held the prestigious post of Aasthana Vidwan (designated official scholar) of Thirupati Thirumala Devaswam. He was the active administrative member of many types of councils like "Sangeetha Naataka Academy", "Madras Music Academy", "University Grants Commission", etc. He was instrumental in selection of eligible music students for scholarships under various programmes of these organisations. Famous veena artists like, Chittibabu, Pappu Someshwara Rao, Emani Kalyani (daughter), V. Saraswathi, Sathyamoorthi, etc., belong to his tutelage. He also introduced the famous playback singer, P. B. Srinivas and brought him to limelight. The following are some of his famous composition symphony:

1. Bhramara Vinyasa (musical depiction of the routine of honeybee).
2. Aadarsha Shikharaarohana.

3. Todi-Raagam-Thaanam-Pallavi.
4. Indu: Six raagas of the first Chakra (cycle) of 72 Melakartha raagas of Venkatamukhi.
5. Bhaaratha Jyothi (In commemoration of Pt. Jawaharlal Nehru).
6. Sowmya Purusha (Biography of Mahatma Gandhi).

He was accorded with many honours and numerous awards like "Padmashri", "Maha Mahopaadhyaya", "Chathurdandi Panditha", "Vainika Shikhamani", "Veena Chakravarthi", "Vallaki Vallabha", "Veena Gaana Gandharva", etc!

Veenai Dhanammal

Dhanammal was born in a musical family in the year 1867 in Chennai. Her mother was the disciple of the great Shyama Shastry's son, Subbaraya Shastry. Dhanammal's grandmother, Kamalakshi, was a famous Bharata Naatyam artist. Dhanammal started learning music and veena rendering under the guidance of her mother and continued the studies under the tutelage of Alasingarayya, Valajapete Balakrishna,(a repository of the padams) and Saatanoor Panchanatha Iyer.

She became popular by the name "Veenai Dhanammal" because of her scholarly knowledge in playing veena and her own style of playing technique which is known by her name, "Dhanammal Baani. This Baani (style) has an excellent gamaka, producing the linking of swaras through vibrating adjacent notes. It also produces the tones of preceding and succeeding notes in the micro sound level. Many vocalists now use this technique to present the profoundness of voice and its richness. Influenced by this style, Thiruvatriyoor Thyaagayya, Dharmapuri Subbaraya, etc. have composed many Varnas, Padams and Javalis in this style and became famous for this style. Granddaughters of Veenai Dhanammal, T.Muktha, T.Brinda, and also many others are famous for singing and presenting this unique style. Veenai Dhanammal passed away in 1938. After her demise, Madras Music Academy of Chennai started Dhanammal Memorial Awards to inspire and encourage the budding and dynamic veena artists. In 2010,

Government of India released postal stamp in commemoration of Veenai Dhanammal.

ThrissurA. Anantha Padmanabhan

An "A Top" AIR artist of excellence, A. Anantha Padmanabhan served All India Radio, Thrissur for 36 years as a veena artist till 2012.

He was born in1951 in Thiruvananthapuram to famous Vainika T.S. Ananthakrishna Iyer. Ananthapadmanabhan learnt veena playing from his father. At the same time, he was attracted by the melody of sitar playing by Pandit Bade Gulam Ali Khan and Pandit Ravishankar and learnt sitar also. Soon, he mastered the sitar playing techniques, as well gained the knowledge of Hindustani Classical music. He started presenting sitar concerts and later devoted his time for veena playing because of the richness, melody, depth and "naada soukhya"(sound-delight) of veena.

At the young age, he used to play sitar and veena in the Orchestra at Thiruvananthapuram, by name "Thunder Birds" and during this time he mastered the style of western music also. When he was pursuing formal education, he spent most of his time in late nights for the innovation and mastering of new techniques of veena playing.

With the in-depth study and knowledge of various veena Baanis (Mysore style, Andhra Style, Karaikkudi Style, S. Balachander Style, etc.), he identified all the excellent techniques in these Baanis. Along-with these selected techniques, he blended the technique of tonal continuity of Hindustani music styles and sitar playing styles thus came up with a unique style, well known by his name. This style produced more gamakas with less plucking and mastery over left hand fingerings. The specialty of his style is to play raaga bhaava (intention of raaga), saahitya bhaava (intention of content of kriti) and thaanams in gaayana (vocal) style and vaadana (playing) styles in the third speed also. Even though he is a B.Sc. mathematics graduate, he is known for presenting the simple flow of melody with importance to raaga and sahithya bhaavas in his concerts.

In 1971, he started to present his veena concerts beginning from the veena recital at Amman temple at Thekkethuruvu. After that, he won the hearts of many music lovers in India, at UNESCO and other countries like France, Germany, Middle East and Gulf countries, Singapore, etc. with over thousands of his fantastic performances of veena recital, sitar recital, Jugalbandhis of these instruments, fusion of rhythm based instruments(laya vaadyams), Western fusion concerts, etc. He got back the dignity and popularity of veena playing techniques in all over the world. S. Bala Chander, Shemmangudi Srinivasa Iyer, M.D. Ramanathan, etc. are his most revered role models. During one of the death anniversaries of S. Baalachander, veena recital concert of Ananthapadmanabhan was organized in Chennai. Shemmangudi Srinivas Iyer celebrated his 90th birthday function with veena concert by this modern time great Vainika.

Already he has composed some vernas and thillaanas (important special items of full-fledged music concerts) which are becoming popular. The specialties of these presentations are, "raaga bhaava, saahithya bhaava, melodies, and minimal calculations without complications in linking the swara-sanchaaras to the pallavis". Every concert is made unforgettable, by his deep involvements in designing the new special items for that day, such as, varieties of thaanam renderings in vilambitha, madhya and dhritha kaalas in three sthaayees, incorporating some Hindustani versions (like Jod-jhaala), Western note-combinations producing peculiar higher harmonic notes in the lower sthaayees, like birds' kuhoo- kuhoo-voices, flute-notes, etc, keeping the audience in rapt attention! His presentation of "Raag Pahaadi"is unmatched! His rendering techniques of any raagas specially, "Kalyaana vasantha, Jai jayavanthi, Nalina kaanthi, Chaaru keshi, Ranjani, Yaman, Kaambhoji, Kaapi (Peelu), Saraswathi, etc, and many others to mention, are superb and have mesmerized the audience!

He has directed music for several Malayalam films and also acted in some films. Compact-discs, albums with vivacious veena concerts, fusion musics, a special presentation of various emotions

in "navarasas" of the earth-mother and Nature expecting the rains, in different raagas - "Varsha-Mohini;"which is suitable for "Mohini-Attams", etc are being published by him.

The musical composition "Saayujya", directed by him, won the first place in the "sangeetha roopaka" competition organized by All India Radio, Prasara Bharathi, New Delhi. He was awarded with honours like Kerala Sangeetha Naataka Academy award, Guruvayurappan Chembai award, and Gaana Kala Thilaka award from the Government of Goa, etc.

His wife, Mrs. Usha, is also an expert veena player. She is also teaching and guiding many veena students. His son, Anand Kaushik, though a software engineer by profession, was also an exponent of veena. He was exhibiting his talent by playing veena- duets with his father and proving his abilities to rise to newer heights in the field of Classical veena recital, enchanting the audience with divine music.

Some of famous Vainikas of India

- ❖ Vainika Shikhamani Veene Sheshanna
- ❖ Veene Saambaiah
- ❖ Veena Bhakshi Chikkaramappa
- ❖ Dodda Sheshanna
- ❖ Veene Subbanna
- ❖ Veene Venkatagiriappa
- ❖ Veene Shaamanna
- ❖ Veene Shivaramaiah
- ❖ Veene Krishnaiah
- ❖ Veenai Dhanammaal
- ❖ Veene Venkataramanadaasa
- ❖ Karaikkudi Subbarama Iyer
- ❖ Karaikkkudi Sambashiva Iyer
- ❖ Emani Achyutarama Shasthry
- ❖ Emani Shankara Shasthry
- ❖ Emani Kalyani
- ❖ Sangameshwara Shasthry
- ❖ S. Balachander

- ❖ R. Venkataraman
- ❖ Anantha Krishna Iyyer
- ❖ A.Anantha Padmanabhan
- ❖ A.Ananda Kaushik
- ❖ Gomathi Chidamberam
- ❖ Deshmangalam Subrahmanya Bhagavathar
- ❖ Karamana Parameshwara Bhagavathar
- ❖ M.K. Kalyana Krishna Bhagavathar
- ❖ M.A. Kalyana Krishna Bhagavathar
- ❖ K.S.Narayana Swamy
- ❖ Bhagya Lakshnmi Chandra Shekhar
- ❖ T.N.Shesha Gopalan
- ❖ Rajalakshmi Tirunarayan
- ❖ M.K. Saraswathi
- ❖ R.N. Doraiswamy
- ❖ V. Doraiswamy Iyengar
- ❖ D. Balakrishna
- ❖ C. Krishnamoorthy
- ❖ Geetha Ramanand
- ❖ Suma Sudheendra
- ❖ Vijaya Raghavan
- ❖ A.S. Padma
- ❖ Kalyani Ganeshan
- ❖ Mysore Rajalakshmi
- ❖ Pudukkottai Krishna Moorthi
- ❖ Ranganayaki Rajagopalan
- ❖ S. Rukmini
- ❖ Prof. Balakrishna Palghat
- ❖ Vidya Shankar
- ❖ Ramanatha Iyer
- ❖ Gopinatha Iyer
- ❖ Manchala Jagannatha Rao
- ❖ Mudigondan Ramesh
- ❖ V.L. Janakiraam
- ❖ Kalpagam Swaminathan

- Rajeshwari Padmanabhan
- Padmavathi Ananthagopalan
- Jayanthi Kumaresh
- S. Sundar
- Revathi Krishnan
- Revathi Srinivasan
- E. Gayathri
- Jayaraj
- Jayashri Jayaraj
- Srividya Chandramouli
- Rajesh Vaidya
- Prince Ramavarma
- R.K. Srinivas Moorthy
- M.J. Srinivasa Iyyengar
- R.K. Raghavan
- R.K. Padmanabha
- R. Vishveshwaran
- Shrimathi Sharada Shivanandam
- Shivanandam
- Chitti Babu
- Pappu Someshwara Rao
- D. Srinivas
- Duddu Seetharamaiah
- R.S. Keshavamoorthy
- Swaramoorthy V.N. Rao
- Mysore V. Subrahmanyam
- Radhika Natarajan
- L. Raja Rao
- T. Sharada
- K.R. Lakshmi Iyyangar, Manipal.
- R. Pichumani Iyer
- Dr. A.P.J. Abdul Kalam (Former President of India!)

* * * * *

Chapter - 10

Raaga Identification and Analysis

(Using, soft-ware technology)

In Carnatic classical music, there are 72 melakartha (Janaka) raagas and about 35,000 (72×22×22=34848!) Janya raagas (theoretically infinite raagas!), derived from melakartha raagas. Out of these only some, about 250 raagas are being practiced and are popular. Decorum of these raagas, the techniques of presentations with many note- vibrations (gamakas), etc. are deeply complicated. Because of this, many find it difficult to differentiate and identify these rare raagas. Music students and music lovers and enthusiasts have to study music incessantly to gain the skill of identifying the raagas. Also, there were no specific measurable criteria to determine the exact scales, notes and purity of shruthi to identify the raagas. Due to these lacunae, opinions of the judges differ drastically during the music competitions or examinations. Also these have become more of subjective skills rather than being objective and accurate. These short comings were overcome by the usage of computer applications to identify the raaga consistencies, purity of tones (shruthi consistencies), etc, Thanks to many physicists who invented software techniques for raaga identification, based on frequencies or pitch of notes.

In music, shruthi is the base pitch or fundamental frequency(n) of vibrations. Pure sound note or swara is a simple harmonic vibration mathematically represented by a sine-wave as instantaneous displacement of the particle, $x = A\,Sine\,2\pi nt$, where n is the frequency of vibration in the fundamental mode, and A is its amplitude (maximum displacement). Along with this, there are its harmonics, overtones and sympathetic vibrations. All these, simple harmonic vibrations of the fundamental frequency and their overtones of different volumes (energy quanta) combine to form a deformed or distorted note (waveform) which is different for different sources of sounds and experienced differently by the listeners as tones or naada (ref: naada and naada-bedha chapter-4). This acoustical energy of vibrations is converted to electrical energy through the microphones. By the use of computer technology, this electrical energy can be obtained in the digital form with the help of Fast Fourier Transfer (FFT) technology based on the Fourier Series Analysis of mathematics. This analysis will give details like, frequency, volume (energy) and levels of fundamental frequencies, sympathetic vibrations and harmonics. With these details, it is possible to classify and identify the scale and volume of each tone and notes. Comparison of these analyzed data against the standard raaga chart and frequency tables, will exactly identify the raaga consistency, shruthi consistency and rhythm accuracy of musical notes of instruments and even of vocal music, presented by the artists!

Analysis of shruthi

From the digitalization of base shruthis (fundamental frequencies) of various popular vocalists, musical instruments, etc., comparison was possible between the scale and volume of sympathetic vibrations and harmonics. This comparison helped to form the standard, considering the specialty variance of each tone. This process of analysis helped to classify tones of large sized instruments like veena, gottuvadyam, bansuri, mridangam, naadaswaram, etc. as Purusha shruthis (base or male-tones) and tones of small instruments like, mandolin, flute, violin, shehanai, etc. as Sthree shruthis (treble or female-tones). Thamboora can be classified into any of these two, depending on the thickness of the strings used (refer: Naada-Delight in chapter- 8).

Analysis of Gamakas

The majesty of Indian classical music lies in the incorporation of highly skilled "gamakas", one kind of decorative presentations of swinging from one note to another with vibrations, into the raaga compositions. Ten gamaka styles were preloaded into single 'swara-note' and was

analyzed with this Raaga Detection Technology. The results were similar to the predicted pattern of frequencies, sympathetic vibrations, harmonics and overtones.

Analysis of swara, raaga

The digitalization of 72 melakartha raagas in veena, rendered by an authoritative veena maestro, S. Balachander, was taken as the basis of purity of swara and raagas with respect to sympathetic vibrations and harmonic overtones based on its range, scale and energy of vibrations. This was compared against the preset raaga structure, as per the defined and standard parameter, to conclude the authenticity of this process. Likewise, recordings of many famous vocalists and instrumentalists were compared against the preset data. Even with the slightest deviation from the authentic raaga structures, the computer software identified them as different raagas!

Purity of Shruthi and Raaga

Some of the most popular raagas like Kalyani, Shubha panthuvarali, Kharahara priya, etc., rendered by various artists were recorded and were analyzed for its binding with the Raaga structure and purity in its Shruthi. The purity (consistency) of shruthi is to the extent of 97% to 99%, and the perfection in raaga structure is only to the tune of 88% to 92% as determined in the case of well known artists. However in these methods, the duration of the testing is too short only three or four minutes, which is not adequate for judging and passing any remarks!

This new technology can be utilized in the practical music examinations or competitions to adjudge the right quality, authenticity and skill of music students or competitors and recognize the right and meritorious candidates.

Please note: for more details, visit internet websites containing: Real Time Raga Detection and Analysis by – James K.N., A Doctoral Thesis.

* * * * *

Chapter - 11

Divine Veena: Its Present Status

Veena vaadana in temples

Temples in India are the soul and strength of Indian philosophy, vedic culture, classical music, classical dances, etc. Temples are the very powerful spiritual centers of the great cultural heritage of India. It is true that, in spite of repeated aggressions and onslaughts by foreigners on our culture, natural treasures, knowledge centers like Universities, India could retain its originality in philosophy, wisdom and cultural values because of numerous temples all over the country. To overcome the tension and mental disturbances caused by the external and socio-economic factors of the materialistic world, people visit temples in search of solace and peace. By meditation and deep devotion, they establish the psychological contact with the God through the deities of temples. For this, the ambience of the temple should be cool, calm and collected. Unpolluted atmosphere and environments of temples can soothen the unwanted emotions and external temptations, thus helping the devotee to have a blissful, spiritual, virtuous life with qualitative contribution to the society at large. Divine and supreme veena, through its melodious, majestic tonal qualities and naada soukhya, adds to the divine ambience of the temples. Perhaps, that is why; veena is shown with the idols of Goddesses, stone sculptures (shila balikas) etc. in temples. Not only this, very much importance should be given to classical music concerts, Bharatha-Naatyams and such unexciting fine arts items especially during the religious festivals. A few examples will certainly justify the contributions of music and Divine veena renderings to the Divinity of the temples. There are many temples and sacred places in India and also in many other countries, where such

programs are regularly conducted. The following are some of such interesting episodes.

Veena rendering service at Sri Ranganatha Swamy temple of Sri Rangam, at Trichy

This is a very famous ancient temple of about 1000 year's history. Sri Ramanujacharya after performing twelve years of spiritual sadhanas (thapasya-penance) at Melkote, Karnataka, returned to Trichy, about 900 years back, laid down specific procedures to be followed in the daily routine and special festival ocasions. Melodious veena playing music and its importance was mentioned frequently in many earlier Tamil literatures of famous Alvaars and such others. Knowing this, Ramanujacharya introduced veena vadana seva in this famous temple at that time. The responsibility was assigned to a Sathyakootam family, a clan living in a village near Sri Rangam. The 45th generation is still continuing this tradition! These details are very interesting and intriguing. Almost for 260 days of the year, Vainikas perform Ekantha veena vaadana seva (veena playing in solitude in front of the Deity) twice a day. Early in the morning at 5.15 a.m to 5.45 a.m. One Vainika plays veena as Suprabhatam morning welcome tunes to awaken! the Lord before the beginning of the daily rituals. Likewise, even at night, after, all the daily rituals, veena is played in solitude, pleasing the Lord to have Shayanam (and go to sleep!). For this, Thondarapodi Alvaar's 10 beautiful-devotional verses had been chosen. These ten verses were broken and rendered in five different raagas, namely: Bhoopali, Bilahari, Dhanyasi, Malaya- Marutha and Saveri. During both these times, there should be total silence in the temple surroundings. Bells or any other music instruments are not allowed to be played during this Ekaantha veena vaadana service! There is a saying in Brihadaaranyaka Upanishad, which means "There should not be any other sound when veena is played!" In line with this, even in this temple, veena is being given high prominence and is used very often, as well as, during the festivities.

Veena vaadana: during Irapattu and Pagalpattu festivals

During the annual festivities at Sri Ranganatha Swamy temple, for 10 days starting from Vaikunta Ekadashi, combined veena recitals of many Vainikas together is being conducted since ages. These, five or more, Vainikas usually from this family, play their veenas synchronized together as a seva (Ritual). Even before the festive procession begins, these Vainikas go on playing many popular compositions. Once, the procession begins from the Thousand Pillar Mantap and reaches Naalikethana Dwaara, they start playing Thaanam in "Ghanapanchaka raagams" i.e. Naata, Gaula, Aarabhi, Varaali and Shri-raagas, and continue to play till the procession reaches the south-west corner of Raja Mahendra Peetham. After this, the "Utsava Moorthy" (deity of procession) is taken through the eight steps to the main temple. During this stage of procession, Vainikas tie their veenas to their waist to keep them vertically while playing. They move climbing these eight steps backwards, facing the deity and simultaneously play Veena! The prescribed composition to be played during this phase of backward procession is "Echcharike sadhanamu ekantha Rangaa" in raaga Yadukula Kambhoji, composed by Vijayaranga Chokkanaatha Naayaka (a musician devotee lived during, 1704- 1731). This has 4 charanas (verses) and each charana is to be played for every two steps. At the same time, there is always a heavy crowd of devotees for the Darshanam of Sri Ranganatha! One can imagine the tremendous pressure on the Vainikas and skill level required to play in a synchronized way in such a difficult situation! The effort and dedication of these Vainikas, who play veena like this, during all these ten days' festive processions, is praise worthy. While this ritual is conducted in the night procession of Irapattu, similar veena rendering service is followed in the noon during the ten days' Pagalpattu festival.

These Vainikas of Srirangam are conducting similar veena vaadana sevas in Ranganaayaki Devi temple and Kamalavalli Devi temples of Urraiyyur, during the four days' festivals every year.

Hundreds of devotees are usually waiting in the temple premises with enthusiasm to listen and get immersed with divinity of Ekantha Veena Vaadana Seva in the perfect silence of both early mornings and late nights. Similarly, people gather in large numbers to get engrossed with the divine music of synchronised many veena playing during the Irapattu and Pagalpattu festivals!

This tradition is still followed by the family of Dr. Rangarajan of Sathyakootam's clan. Dr. Rangarajan was a Professor of physics and sometimes Vice-Principal, of Trichy National College. He and many of his family members: father, uncles, children and even grand-children are very good Vainikas! He was performing the Ekantha veena vadana service for a long time of about 71 years, from 1940 to 2011! All his family members are committed, integral part in continuing this noble Ekantha veena vadana seva, the Irapattu and Pagalpattu festivals in Sri Ranganatha Swamy Temple.

Likewise, in a Shiva Temple at Vaikam near Kottayam, Veena Vaadana Seva is being performed every evening during the "Deepotsava" since many centuries. There could be even more temples having this ritual and tradition of Veena Vaadana Seva, and there is a need to collect, compile and document such cultural heritages.

The present status in India and outside countries

Many musicologists, students and music lovers have begun to realize the divine, most melodious veena naadas, in the everyday hectic life under heavy pressures. Still only very few veena concerts, veena festivals are organized. In most of the music festivals veena concerts are very rare! But here are the few exceptions:

1. Department of veena, Sri Swaathi Thirunal Maharaja College of Music, Thiruvanandapuram (Kerala), is conducting three days' workshop on veena rendering techniques, "Sadhana" every year.
2. Sri Guru Guha Vaggeya Prathistana Trust with Sri Guru Guha Sangeetha Maha Vidyalaya, Shimoga (Karnataka), an institution

for Carnatic classical music, is organizing veena concerts, for a week, "Veena Mahotsava Sapthaha", every year with the participation of many reputed Vainikas throughout the country.

3. Veenothsavas of short time durations are conducted in New Delhi, Chennai and few other places. Some temples at Madurai, Coimbatore etc also conduct multi (group) veena rendering concerts during the Navarathri festival periods, etc.

4. Recently, in many temples, the celestial divine sound "OM" the mother of all musical sounds, as produced by a thamboora or Om Namha Shivaya in Shiva temples, Om Gam Ganapathaye Namha in Ganesh temples etc. are played continuously, 24 hours, using electronic devices. All will agree that this induces a calm spiritual atmosphere, helping the visiting devotes to cool down their perturbed minds and concentrate better while praying the Almighty.

5. There are many music institutions in Chicago (United States) training in veena, classical vocal music, violin, flute, Bharatha Natyam, etc. Many students are studying veena. They conduct music festivals in a Hindu temple every year in which, about hundreds veena students, more than 200 other instrumentalist, and vocalist participate!

6. Instituions for veena, flute, vocal music etc, in other countries.

Since about fifty years, many foreigners are showing deep interest in our spiritual philosophies, yoga, and culture and study our Indian classical music, vocal, veena, flute, Bharatha Naatyam etc. They have realized the importance of these, in the modern situation of heavy stresses and strains of the socio- economic pressures as very effective methods for stress relief and mental relaxations and visit our country. Recently, many professionalists in these areas, have established training institutions and organizations of various kinds, in United States, Canada, South America, Great Britain and in many European countries (France, Germany, Italy, etc). Most of the institutions and individuals in these countries, claim teaching veena, flute, violin Indian classical music, varieties of percussion instruments, dances, etc, and are flourishing very well!

An in-depth study, analysis and evaluation of all the facts and figures detailed in the foregoing, will certainly lead us to opine that veena is the Emperor of all musical instruments. It is Divine. It is scientific. It is pure. It is blissful. It is complete Supreme. It is our national emblem for fine arts. It is our responsibility and obligation to protect and spread the knowledge of Divine Veena Science.

* * * * *

Bibliography

1. Veena: Instrument par excellence, and its Kannada version, by Vainika Vidwan C.K. Shankara Narayana Rao.
2. Parameshwara's Veena Lakshana. A critical study "Vimarshe" by Dr. Ra. Sathya Narayana, in Kannada.
3. Bharathiya Vaadyagalu, by Prof. A.N. Purandare in Kannada.
4. Veene Sheshanna Bhavana – Souvenir-1991
5. Real Time Raaga Detection and Analysis – Doctoral thesis by James K.N

The readers may also refer the following original literatures for more information and details

1. Sangeetha Rathnakara, by Saranga Deva (12th century).
2. Chathurdandi Prakashike, by Venkatamukhi (17th century).
3. Swara-mela Kalanidhi, by Rama Amathya.
4. Sangeetha Sampradaya Pradarshini, by Subba Rama Dikshither (19th century).
5. Sandhya-Vandana Rahasya and Veda Prakashike (Veena Rahasya), by Yedathore. Subbaraya Sharma (1936).
6. Music of India, by H.A.Popley (1935).
7. History of Indian music, by Prof. P.Samba Murthy.
8. Musical Instruments of India, by S. Krishna Swamy.
9. Viveka Chinthamani, by Sri Nijaguna Shivayogi. Etc.

* * * * *

Parents of Manipal Aruna Kumari

Prof. Shama Bhat & Late Mrs. Haimavathi S. Bhat

Devoted Teachers

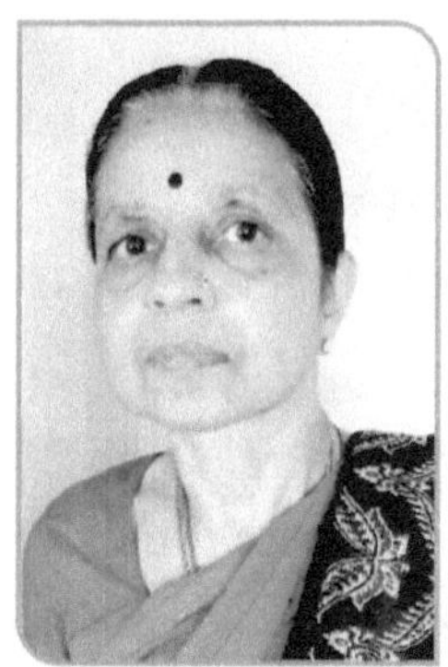

Late Vidwan
Udupi Vasudeva Bhat

Late Vidhushi
K R Lakshmi Iyengar

Gana kala thilak -
Thrissur A Ananthapadmanabhan

Aruna Kumari's family members